ABOUT THE A

John Harrison, who has been described as 'Britain's greatest allotment authority' (*Independent on Sunday*) lives in the north-west of England with his wife Val. They grow their own fruit and vegetables on two allotments which provide much of the food they eat. They also enjoy their own homemade bread, butter, jams and chutneys, as well as home reared eggs, and often drink their own beer and wine.

John runs two popular websites: **www.allotment.org.uk** and **www.lowcostliving.co.uk**. He is the author of three other books in the *Right Way* series: **The Essential Allotment Guide, Low-Cost Living** and, together with Val, **Easy Jams, Chutneys and Preserves**.

PRAISE FOR
VEGETABLE GROWING MONTH BY MONTH

'Harrison's book is crammed with useful information, unencumbered by any trendy graphics . . . it's perfect for all those gardeners who just want a book to tell them exactly what to do, and when.'
Emma Townshend in the *Independent on Sunday*

'Forget about any glossy pictures, what's in this book is solid words of advice, written in plain-to-understand English from a grower who's had frustrating years of experience behind him in trying to grow nutritious vegetables, whilst at the same time running a business and raising a family. Everyone will benefit from this book and I found the glossary at the back, which explains gardening terminology in a way that everyone will understand, to be extremely useful. It will certainly have a place on my extensive gardening bookshelf.'
Medwyn Williams, *Chairman of the National Vegetable Society and member of the Fruit and Vegetable Committee of the Royal Horticultural Society*

VEGETABLE GROWING MONTH BY MONTH

John Harrison

ROBINSON

ROBINSON

First published in Great Britain by Robinson in 2008

Copyright © John Harrison, 2008

10

The moral right of the author has been asserted.

A CIP catalogue record for this book is available from the British Library.

ISBN: 978-0-7160-2189-6 (paperback)
ISBN: 978-0-7160-2244-2 (ebook)

Printed and bound in Great Britain by Clays Ltd., St Ives plc

Constable
is an imprint of
Constable & Robinson Ltd
100 Victoria Embankment
London EC4Y 0DY

An Hachette UK Company
www.hachette.co.uk

www.constablerobinson.com

CONTENTS

INTRODUCTION

It was when I first set up my allotment website that I became aware of how many people were growing their own vegetables for the first time. I realized from the questions being asked on the website's forum that most people nowadays don't have the benefit of following in a parent's or grandparent's footsteps to guide them, as modern society spreads our family across the country and no longer is growing your own vital to full bellies of a night.

These new vegetable growers were looking for a simple, straightforward guide, written in plain English, that told them what to do, when to do it and how to do it. This is what I have tried to provide here.

I'm just an ordinary grower – albeit with 30 years of failure and success under my belt – so I know the difficulties of holding down a job, raising a family and trying to keep a vegetable plot productive and weed-free.

If there is one trick to this, it is 'little and often'. Just half an hour with a hoe one evening, half an hour sowing and potting up the next evening is far better than planning an entire day in the garden at the weekend when it will invariably decide to rain or the family wants a day out or, worse still, the pressures of the job demand some overtime.

That half hour a day, or better still an hour, becomes your

chance to wind down and return to the family refreshed.

If you have children, do try and involve them. The wonder of seeing a seed turn into a plant, and then a crop that finally appears on the plate, is a fantastic cure for the 'I only eat chips and nuggets' disease that is sweeping the nation, its symptoms being obesity and a detachment from the real world in favour of over-developed thumbs pressing the fire button in the latest video game.

That said, do remember that children have shorter attention spans and demand attention themselves. Spend ten minutes teaching them how to hoe and accept that the odd plant is going to be killed by friendly fire. When they get bored, which they will, move onto another job and when they've had enough of the garden let them go back in. It must be fun if they are to discover the joy of gardening and build a life interest.

I've tried to answer the main general questions I am asked but one section of the book above all the rest was very difficult to write: the month by month guide. There is no such thing as an absolute set date for a job in gardening. For a start, temperatures vary according to where you are in the country. Winter comes earlier to Scotland than Devon and a drive from north to south in spring will show that clearly, with bare-branched trees changing to buds and leaves as you travel across the land.

I live in Cheshire which is about half way up the country and have based my guide on this. What I cannot guide you through is the weather. We hear of climate change daily in the news and there is no doubt that the weather is becoming more extreme. We cannot say any individual summer or storm is due to climate change but the pattern is definitely changing.

Unfortunately, we're not rejoicing in a Mediterranean climate with glorious sunshine. The changes are as likely to bring us a cold wet summer as a drought; winter is less likely to bring a freeze and snow but next year it may. All this means we must adapt to the conditions and be more aware and prepared for the extremes.

So read the month by month guide with an eye on the outside world. Even in 'the good old days', that were never quite as good as they seem in hindsight, the real skill of the gardener was being able to adapt to the changing weather conditions. It is surprising how often late plantings will catch up and I've had just as much success, in fact more, with parsnips planted in April rather than February as those old books advised.

You will have failures, that's part of growing. As I write at the end of a summer that has been the wettest recorded and, by general agreement, the worst in memory for the vegetable grower, we still have managed to cover most of our needs.

This year farmers struggled with blight, which thrives and spreads when the weather is warm and damp. Despite a truly awesome chemical weapons array, many lost their potato crop. But I grew the new Hungarian Sarpo variety which is not only resistant to blight but seems to be unpalatable to the slugs, another pest that enjoyed the damp conditions.

These new resistant crops promise the ability to get results without the reliance on chemicals of the previous generation, which is just as well since many are no longer available as stringent safety testing has seen their withdrawal from the amateur armoury. This is no bad thing because a major benefit of growing your own is the certain knowledge that your vegetables are free of poisonous pesticide residues. That's not to say this is yet another organic growing book, as I do believe there are times where the use of weedkillers and chemical fertilizers make sense – but the choice, of course, is yours.

I hope you find this book of value and enjoy it. Of necessity it is only a primer but I hope it encourages and enables you to grow your own.

1

WHY GROW YOUR OWN VEGETABLES?

There are many reasons why people grow their own and I'll try to cover the main ones here. It's difficult to say what will encourage you into home growing but I expect you'll find that some of the following apply to you.

The economics of vegetable growing are tempting as long as you don't cost your own labour and, even there, you can consider the exercise as a saving on the expense of going to a gym. A packet of seeds can cost as little as 50p and produce vegetables worth many pounds; a considerable saving, especially when compared with the cost of organic vegetables.

In fact, if you are on a tight budget and have spare time, you can make a significant reduction in a family's food budget. The average allotment plot of ten poles has been calculated to produce over £800 worth of fruit and vegetables at shop prices in a year, enough to feed a family of four. A pole, by the way, is a traditional measurement of land equivalent to about 25 square metres. Costs vary but, at the time of writing, usually range from £20 to £40 per annum for renting an allotment.

More important to many people than a cost saving is the knowledge of what has actually gone into their food and the benefits to the environment in general. Certainly the 'air miles' that attach to food from the supermarket add to our carbon footprint and ultimately harm the environment of our planet.

One supermarket was found to sell salad crops that were locally grown within five miles of the store but after being harvested were transported to an airport from where they were flown to Poland for cleaning and packaging before being flown back, transported to a distribution centre and then by road to the store. A round trip of hundreds of miles for a lettuce grown within five miles of the shop!

Compare that with the ecological cost of sending a packet of seeds by post and walking the produce to a kitchen from the plot. Growing your own also saves the cost of packaging food. Less plastic in the landfill has to be a good thing.

Even when you can source your vegetables locally there is always a concern about what the food contains. Forty-three per cent of all shop-bought vegetables and fruit contain detectable levels of pesticides. Even though these may be within government safety guidelines, the safety testing of pesticides assumes a healthy adult and doesn't take into account vulnerable groups such as the elderly, infirm, young and unborn.

There is also the 'cocktail effect' with pesticide residues. Studies have shown that three pesticides consumed together equal up to one hundred times the effect of any one on its own. It is practically impossible to test all the possible combinations of these residues and other additives for safety.

Scandals regarding food sold as organic, and free range eggs that turned out not to be, have further damaged confidence in the food we buy.

By growing your own you take control of your food and know its provenance. Even if you use pesticides or fungicides on your own produce, you know how much has been used and, I hope, will minimize that use. Most home growers tend not to use pesticides and fungicides at all, even if they would not qualify as organic gardeners.

Fully organic gardeners use no herbicides, no chemical

fertilizers and very few pesticides and fungicides from an approved range. Whichever system you favour, by growing your own, you will be in control of your food.

One area in which shop-bought food, organic or not, cannot compete with home grown is freshness and taste. The taste of sweetcorn picked and cooked just minutes later is incomparable. The moment the cob is picked, the sugars start to change to starch and the sweetness is being lost. Freshly picked new potatoes are a delight to the tastebuds, not just a filler on the plate. I've seen children, who normally treat vegetables as if they were poison on their plate, happily eat tomatoes from the plant and peas from the pod.

When a farmer chooses what variety to grow, he looks at a number of factors: yield, suitability for his soil and microclimate, regular shape to fit into the supermarket specifications, whether the crop will ripen at the same time to make harvest easier, how long it can be stored, how easily it will stand up to being transported and, finally, if at all, taste.

When you grow your own, you can choose varieties that farmers would not grow. Not just varieties that taste well but varieties that you personally prefer the taste of. Varieties that mature over a longer period and so provide fresh crops over a period of time. No longer limited to red or white potatoes or Jersey Royals, you can pick from over four hundred varieties of the humble potato. Tomatoes with thin skins that would never make it to the supermarket in saleable condition will easily make it home from the vegetable plot.

And don't forget that whilst you are growing your own food you're getting healthy exercise and fresh air without paying a subscription to a gym club. In fact, there have been studies that show gardening is good for your mental health as well. Working with the soil is good for the soul, as well as the muscles.

Finally, there is the fun and satisfaction you can get from growing your own. It really is hard to explain the feeling you experience when you sit down to a meal where the vegetables started as a packet of seeds in your hand. When you have not grown your own, a cauliflower may not seem a big deal but just you wait until it is *your* cauliflower and you have nurtured it from a seedling, and fought against marauding hordes of slugs and caterpillars to bring it safely through to maturity. That is when you get a real feeling of pride.

Most vegetable growers purely grow for the table but you might find you enjoy showing off your vegetables as well. There are literally hundreds of shows every year ranging from village halls to prestigious national shows like Harrogate where the crème de la crème of vegetable growers show the results of their labours.

2

WHERE TO GROW AND PREPARING TO GROW

One thing I have heard said many times is, 'I'd love to grow my own but I haven't anywhere to grow.' The truth is that you don't need a huge garden in which to grow your own vegetables. I've a friend in a third floor flat who grows salad crops, tomatoes, carrots and beans on her balcony and even managed red cabbages in a pot.

With a space of just ten square metres, about the size of a very small patio, you can provide a couple with many of the vegetables for the table. Throw in some large pots on the patio and you can even have potatoes as well.

The ideal vegetable plot is south-facing and sunny, without overhanging or shading trees and bushes. Do not expect much from a plot under a tree whose leaves collect the sun's energy from above and whose roots take the water and nutrients from below, leaving little or nothing for your crops.

We expect an awful lot from our vegetable bed so do try to give them prime position. Avoid frost pockets at the base of a slope as this will reduce your growing season.

If you don't want to give up space in a garden to a vegetable plot, you can always grow some vegetables in your flower borders. This *potager* style of growing was made popular in France where often the vegetable plot is set out in a decorative style rather than in the conventional British style of rows in a rotation order.

You can even set up a vegetable border that is every bit as attractive as a flower border. Just like with a flower border, you use the attributes like height and colour in your plan.

The old variety of runner bean, Painted Lady, was originally grown as a decorative rather than a food plant. Running them up a trellis at the back of a border, with decorative cut and come again lettuce in the front, makes an attractive display that is edible as well.

Container Growing

When we found ourselves in a house with a concrete-covered backyard, we managed to grow significant amounts of our vegetables and salads in containers.

Nearly anything that will grow in open ground can be grown in a container and often more successfully. The expert show-growers with their huge and perfect leeks, carrots and cabbages would not think of growing in the soil; it is all container grown.

Growing in containers does require some different techniques from growing in the ground and a little more attention to detail. Obviously you are limited in space and will be demanding a lot from a little soil, so the first rule is to fill the containers with a good quality general purpose compost. You can buy this quite cheaply in bags from the DIY or garden centre. Do go for the best quality you can afford; some of the cheapest composts are coarse and lacking in nutrients. Humax is a good brand that I have found to be consistently good.

Because you are growing vegetables, which like their soil to be less acid than most flowers, a little lime added to the compost will be beneficial. If you have a pH meter or soil test kit, you can measure the acidity of the compost and calculate how much lime to add. A pH (the measurement of acidity) of around 6 is great for most vegetables, although the cabbage family prefer around 7. Potatoes dislike lime so do not add lime to their compost.

Now the compost will contain enough nutrients to get your plants started but after a month it will be running out of steam. You will need to add some extra fertilizer to get the best results. For most vegetables, a controlled release fertilizer, such as those sold for hanging baskets, will be ideal or you can add controlled amounts of liquid fertilizer throughout the season.

Just as with the compost, it is worthwhile going for a quality fertilizer. Although all general fertilizers contain the basic elements for growing, the better quality fertilizers contain trace elements as well. Just like vitamins for us, these trace elements are essential for healthy growth.

The size of the container is important. There is no point trying to grow parsnips or carrots in a shallow container since they require depth to grow so I would look for a container at least 30cm (12 inches) deep for those. The area of the container is the next constraint and that will depend on the crop grown.

Growbags are a cheap and easy way to grow tomatoes, peppers and cucumbers but you can greatly improve their performance by increasing their volume. If you take a plant pot (a 15cm/6 inch or 20cm/8 inch diameter plastic pot is ideal) and cut off the bottom to form a tube this can be set into the growbag, with the top of the tube sticking out of the top of the growbag, and thereby providing greater depth to plant in. Just fill it with the compost from inside another growbag.

Don't forget with container growing that regular watering is vital. Unlike growing in the soil where there is usually some reserve below the surface to get the plants through a dry spell, with container growing there is no reserve. It may seem crazy, but you will find you even need to water when it is raining, otherwise the plants will die of thirst.

Do not try and get around this by flooding one day and forgetting the next: that results in burst tomatoes and cracks in carrots, etc. Your containers should also allow excess water to drain because, just like us, plants can drown. If you pierce your growbag with a skewer about 2.5cm (1 inch) above ground level, this will allow excess water to drain away whilst holding a reserve at the base.

Most vegetables need full sun to give of their best, so position your containers in the sunniest spot possible. Shade deprives the plants of sunlight which is what provides the energy for their growth. The more sun, the better they will grow for you.

What to Grow in Containers

There are a few crops that really aren't suitable for containers – sweetcorn and Jerusalem artichokes for example – but most others will do well. What you do need to do is to select the right variety of each plant. If you look for vegetables that state 'suitable for close spacing' or 'close planting' and are sometimes described as 'mini veg', then these will tolerate the space restriction.

Since you are going to change the compost next year, you need not worry about crop rotation. The interplanting of different things close in pots (you could have leeks, spring onions, lettuce and carrots all together, for example) seems to confuse many pests as well. As faster growing crops like lettuce are used, it frees more space for the slower growing crops.

Some varieties you can try:

Saladings

Suitable lettuce varieties would be Tom Thumb or Little Gem. Or you could sow a mixed baby leaf collection and make your salads more varied. Cut and come again varieties will provide a continuous supply.

Interplant with some salad onions and radish and you have the makings of a really fresh salad.

Carrots

You can get some really nice clean young carrots from a container. Good varieties for container growing are Amsterdam Forcing or Early Nantes 2. Sweet young carrots go well in a salad or just wash and steam them to go with a hot meal. Try station sowing about five seeds to the station and thinning to one or just scatter the seeds and use the thinnings whole in salads. Station sowing just means sowing seed at their final spacing and then thinning to one plant after germination.

Potatoes

You can get a surprising amount from growing in pots or even just plastic sacks. It's important to feed well and one trick I heard was to plant one seed potato per pot. When ready, take the plant from the pot, remove enough potatoes for one meal from the plant and replace in the pot. Leave for a month (continuing to feed and water) and there will be another meal in the pot. With a number of pots you can take from one and then the next, giving you a meal every day.

It's only worth using fast first early varieties such as Swift or Rocket for container growing.

Broad, French and Runner Beans

Most dwarf French beans will perform well in a pot but for broad beans you need a dwarf variety, such as The Sutton, and for the runner beans a variety such as Hestia, which is not a climbing variety and will perform well in a pot. I have grown normal runner beans in a large tub but the dwarf varieties are more sensible if space is really tight.

Leeks

Any ordinary variety should be fine but you will need to keep the point where the leaves meet the shaft collared to get a good blanch (the white stem part of the leek) as you will not be able to deep plant in a hole. A cardboard toilet roll centre will do the trick.

Onions

I've not tried ordinary onions because I doubt they are worth it in a limited space but there is no reason why you shouldn't be able to grow them. Close spacing of onions will result in smaller bulbs but that applies to onions on a conventional plot. Spring onions are ideal for a container system.

Cabbage

Try something like April or Chirimen F1 or F1 Hispi or Pixie which are ideal for close spacing and container growing. I have seen three grown from a 30cm (12 inch) diameter bowl!

Cauliflower

You can try Avalanche F1, which is particularly good for solid miniature heads, just enough for a meal.

Beetroot, Turnips

For beetroot try Pablo F1 and for turnips try Arcoat or Snowball.

Tomatoes

Tomatoes are often grown in pots or growbags on a patio but you can do really well with them in a hanging basket. Try the Balconi Collection from Thompson & Morgan or my favourite Gartenpearle (Garden Pearl). Putting a marigold into the pot not only looks good but also helps to deter whitefly, a pest on tomato plants.

Raised Deep Beds

In recent years, raised beds have become a popular method of growing. They first became popular in the 1970s where the soil was mounded between paths and more vegetables could be grown on the rounded surface. Unfortunately, heavy rain would wash the bed onto the paths and defeated the object of the exercise.

Converts to deep bed growing soon moved onto walled

sides to their deep bed, losing the benefit of the additional area, which was not much anyway, but gaining the stability of walled construction.

Before constructing deep beds you should really consider if they are the right thing for you. Weigh the advantages and disadvantages carefully before going into construction.

Advantages and Disadvantages of Raised Bed Growing

Constructing deep beds correctly is hard work and can be quite costly in terms of materials but once done they are easy to maintain and should last for many years.

Yield per square foot is higher with a deep bed but the space taken up by paths means that it is generally equal to ordinary growing methods.

Because of the closer planting with deep beds, weeds are suppressed but they still require weeding and this is usually done by hand, which takes longer than hoeing a conventional row. However, psychologically, deep beds are easier to keep in order as you can select and clear a bed at a time rather than coping with a whole plot.

Not all vegetables are ideal for deep beds and for some vegetables you will probably need to select varieties that are suitable for close spacing just as for container growing.

Deep beds can be ideal for purpose-made large cloches and fleece supports (see page 45).

Raised beds generally enable you to create high quality areas of deep topsoil if your soil is poor but they are a lot of effort if you have a good quality soil to start with.

Deep beds can be very attractive and enhance a garden situation where a normal vegetable plot would look out of place. You can even purchase purpose-made kits of wood complete with finials, etc. to construct a decorative raised bed. Raised beds are, once the hard work of construction is done, easier to maintain and they enable those less physically able to continue growing vegetables when they are not up to digging over large plots.

Constructing Raised Deep Beds

The main point of deep beds is that you never tread on them and compact the soil so it is important that you can easily reach into the centre from the side of the bed. The best width will be around 1.2 metres (4 feet) to allow that.

If the bed is too long, then getting to the other side will involve a long walk and you will be tempted to step over the bed, so about 3 metres (10 feet) long is considered the maximum length for convenience.

The main paths will need to be between 60cm and 75cm wide (between 24 and 30 inches wide) to allow easy access with a wheel barrow, with the secondary paths around 45cm (18 inches) wide to allow walking and kneeling as you lean over the bed.

First, plan out where the beds are going and use some line to mark out. Don't be tempted to squeeze the paths; you will regret it. It's better to have a narrow bed because you will not be able to get to the bed with too narrow a path.

Having marked out and checked that you are happy with the layout, you can produce a cutting list for the wood for the sides. One good source can be second-hand scaffolding planks if they are in reasonable condition. Do not use wood that is too thin, like floorboards, because it will rot and be too flimsy to hold the pressure the soil will exert upon it.

Boards the size of 225mm x 38mm are near perfect. Fix them to stout internal corner posts – fence posts can be ideal – with non-rusting screws. Because the wood is in touch with the ground it will be prone to rot so paint with a preservative like Cuprinol, and soak the corner posts, for a long life. The corner posts can be sunk a few inches into the ground to improve stability.

One good idea is to have a finial decorative ball fixed on the top of the corners, like they use for the main posts on stairs. Not only do they look really good but they help when you pull a hosepipe through to a bed, stopping it from dragging across the plants.

Now, and this is important, before you put the wooden frame into position you need to double dig (see page 30) the bed, removing any perennial weed roots and incorporating lots of organic matter like compost or manure into the base of the trench. Break the soil up well as you do this.

Position and level the base using a spirit level. Allow the soil to settle for a few days and then incorporate compost into the top, bringing the soil level up to about 2.5cm (1 inch) below the top of the boards.

Once the beds are in place, it is time to complete the paths between them. Level them out and compact them if loose. A shuffle walk up and down can do this. The easiest thing to do is to buy some porous, weed-suppressant fabric material. Cut to size and lay over the paths and then cover with bark or wood chippings.

I have seen paths made from concrete slabs. If you use these, check the sizing accurately when you position the beds and save yourself a lot of work later. Other materials you can use are gravel and even block paving bricks.

Your raised deep beds are now ready to plant.

Preparing the Vegetable Patch

Your first job is to decide where to grow your vegetables. In an ideal world you will have a patch of good, deep, fertile soil, close to the house and south facing. Reality is likely to fall short of that.

If you haven't got a large garden, or even any garden, then what about an allotment? To track down a site try your local council who will usually know where they are. Some sites are managed by the council and some are self-managed. If you call down to the site on a Sunday morning you're bound to see people there who can give you some information.

Despite what you may have heard, many sites do have vacancies and will be pleased to rent you a plot for a very modest charge. Even if there is a waiting list, it is worth talking to people on the allotment. You may find someone ready to give up or share a plot with you.

Not all plots are equal. Once again, ask existing plotholders what they think about the plots before choosing one. On our small site some plots are wet (being on a down slope), some are sunny and well worked and some are real lemons where nothing has grown but weeds for years.

If you are converting a patch of land or taking over an allotment covered in weeds, take a few minutes to look at what weeds are growing there. Lush tall weeds indicate that the soil is fertile, and weeds such as nettles and docks tell you that it is acidic which will need to be dealt with.

Clearing a large patch of land (the average allotment is 250 square metres) is a daunting task. Rome wasn't built in a day and you need to take your time as well. The ground is going to be the foundation for many years of growing.

One thing you really should never do is run a Rotavator over a patch of weedy ground. The perennial weeds will grow from a root fragment and so chopping them up and tilling the soil is a great way to propagate them and ensure you have a plot absolutely covered in weeds a few weeks later.

The easiest way to clear a weed-covered plot of land is to spray with a glyphosate-based weedkiller like Roundup™. This is absorbed by the plant's leaves and taken down to the roots, thereby killing the weeds, but it is made harmless when it gets to the ground, so enabling planting to take place quickly.

One application, *if applied as per instruction*, is usually sufficient to take care of most weeds although some perennial weeds may require a second application or just digging out by hand. Don't spray one day and dig the next, leave for at least a fortnight, preferably four weeks, to let the weedkiller be taken down to the roots to do its job.

If you are an organic grower and are set against using a herbicide, then you have a harder job to clear the patch in short order. First decide how much time and energy you have.

There is no way I could clear a plot in one go or even one week. You can cover sections of the plot with thick plastic, carpets or tarpaulins (if you have them) and this will hold back growth until you can get to the section. If you leave an area covered for a year or so, then most of the weeds will die.

Personally, I do not want areas out of production that long so I just use covering as a holding method; neither do I think it ecologically sound to have large areas covered with plastic. Some allotments now ban the use of old carpets for this as too many people move on leaving the carpets behind for others to dispose of.

Now take a small section at a time; looking down 30 metres (100 feet) of weeds is enough to make anyone despair. I found 2-metre patches (5 metres wide) – 8 feet and 16 feet wide – to be about right for a day but those younger and fitter can do more.

Start by taking off the surface grasses and short-rooted weeds with a spade – the resulting 'turfs' can be stacked so that they eventually form a loam. If you are converting a lawn into a vegetable patch, then mow it short first and then remove the turf. Stack face down and cover with a tarpaulin or plastic sheeting. After six months you will have a wonderful growing medium.

The deeper rooted perennials (like docks) need their roots digging out. These are the devil to deal with because if you just add them to a cool compost heap they happily grow on. You can try chopping them (to weaken them) and add them to a hot compost heap but a more effective method is drowning in a barrel of water for three weeks or tying up in a plastic bin bag for a few months.

Having completed clearing, the next job is to dig over with a fork. The purpose is to break up the soil and extract any weed roots. Watch out for bindweed – this is one that spreads from a small bit of root. A small stem is probably growing from a foot of tubular white root snaking along a few inches below the surface.

One exception to the rule is mare's tail or horsetail. This

wonderful weed has roots that go down to Hades, well 1.5 metres (5 feet) anyway. The only thing for you to do is try repeated applications of glyphosate-based weedkiller. The problem with this is that you will effectively have the land out of production for a season as you keep repeating the process. It's not officially approved for organic growers.

Now you have the weeds clear you can judge the type and quality of your soil.

Know Your Soil

Soils come in different types and how you work them will depend on this. Soil is formed by years of rocks being split into small particles by the action of water, frost and friction combined with decayed vegetable matter and animal remains. The vegetable matter is known as humus and is vital to the life of the soil. This is what feeds the millions of bacteria and thousands of worms who work tirelessly in your soil to make it productive.

Your soil is the basis of everything you grow and the difference between success and failure lies in the soil. A gardener with a good soil will find his crops forgiving of mistakes in cultivation but a gardener with a poor soil has a struggle to produce good crops whatever he does.

Different Types of Soil

Sandy Soils, as the name suggests, are predominantly sand. Sand is actually relatively large particles of rock which means they do not stick together well and make the soil light and easy to work. It also makes the soil very free-draining, which is a boon in periods of wet weather. The soil warms quickly in spring and is especially good for early crops.

The problem with a sandy soil is that it does not retain water in dry weather and neither does it retain nutrients well. The way to counter this is to add large quantities of animal manure, especially from cows on straw or strawy horse manure and compost.

Clay Soils are made from very fine particles which stick together well. Clay holds water, which is a benefit in dry weather but the opposite in wet. In hot weather the surface may form a hard crust and, when dug, the large clods set like concrete. Often a clay topsoil will have a pan of solid clay underneath which prevents drainage, resulting in waterlogging and lifeless soil.

It's not all bad news with clay soils, though, for they can be amongst the most productive with work. Double digging in the autumn and allowing the winter frosts to break up the clods will help but, as with a sandy soil, the real answer is loads of organic matter. If there is a pan of solid clay underlying the top soil, try to break this up when double digging to allow the water to drain away. If this is impossible, due to the depth of the pan, then consider drainage to get excess water away.

Clay soils tend to be acidic and require lime but the good news is that liming encourages flocculation (the forming of lumps) amongst the fine particles and so makes the soil more workable.

The addition of sharp sand, that is gritty sand rather than fine building sand, will also assist in opening the soil, thereby improving drainage and aeration, and allowing better root growth. Sharp sand is also known as concreting sand and can be obtained delivered in bulk from builders' merchants. Garden centres stock horticultural sands, which are much the same but more expensive.

Chalk Soils are usually very thin and difficult to work without mixing in the chalk layer below. The answer is to build up the soil with organic matter but where the soil is really shallow, sometimes as thin as 150mm, the best answer is to build raised deep beds.

Peaty Soils are the reverse of the soils above, in that they are rich in humus and have a great texture but the process that creates them usually means they are wet and acid. The answer is to dig over to add air and break up the texture whilst adding lime to reduce the acidity. They may also be lacking in nutrients so a programme of adding animal manure and fertilizers will be beneficial.

The Ideal Soil is made from one of the difficult soils above over a period of years. It is deep, easy to work, smooth, soft and loose in texture, is well drained but holds moisture in dry periods and has a lot of humus which is known by the large number of worms living in the soil.

To maintain the soil in this condition compost, manure and lime is added in a regular programme with digging over as required.

The Subsoil. If you dig down through your soil, you will notice a distinct change at some point as you go down. On a clay soil, the change will be from a dark colour to a lighter brown or even blue-tinged colour and more solid texture. On chalk, it will change to a white-coloured layer. Whatever your soil type this layer, known as the subsoil, will be obviously lifeless.

Your task is to increase the depth of top soil above this layer which is where the plant roots gain their sustenance but you cannot just dig up the subsoil in one go. With a shallow soil you should seek to add around 5cm (2 inches) a year by just breaking up the surface of the subsoil and adding organic matter to it. Over the year the worms will feed on that organic matter, pulling the subsoil through their guts and converting it to top soil.

Gardening is a long-term process and each year, with proper cultivation, your soil will improve and the crops it produces improve.

Why, When and How to Dig

Each year, as the season comes to a close, you will see gardeners digging over their plots. You may have heard of 'no dig' growing (see later in this chapter) and wonder why they go to all this trouble.

The reason is that digging improves the texture of the top

soil, assisting drainage and bringing nutrients from below to the surface, thereby encouraging worms and bacterial action. Digging also exposes pests hiding in the soil. Many gardeners will know the experience of being followed down the row as they dig by a robin happily partaking of the exposed bounty.

Digging is carried out in the autumn and early winter months for two reasons. The first is that you do not have crops in the ground so it is free and the second is that the winter freeze and thaw will help to break down the soil into a fine texture, or tilth as we call it, for next year.

With an ideal soil, digging is not needed every year as the action of cultivation, digging up root crops and so forth is already cultivation enough. Even so, double digging on a three to five year cycle will ensure that a hard pan does not develop below the surface.

In those years when you do not need to dig, you can use a green manure to hold the nutrients over winter and provide valuable humus for next year. Of course, the action of digging in the green manure will be cultivation of itself.

With raised deep beds where you never walk on the surface, the action of normal cultivation will be sufficient and apart from the occasional light forking over of the surface no digging is usually required.

Digging should not be carried out when the soil is wet and sticking to your boots as it will pancake and compact. Neither do you want it too dry as it will tend to 'shingle' as fast as it is dug.

There are three main systems of digging: (1) single or plain digging; (2) double digging, which is also known as bastard trenching, possibly because of the effect on your back; and (3) trenching.

Single Digging
This is the easiest form of digging and for good worked soil perfectly adequate for most years. It is a fairly easy action and, once you have the rhythm, quite fast.

Divide the area you intend to dig into two rows. From one row remove a trench of soil one spit deep to the side. A 'spit' is the depth of your spade's blade, about 25cm (10 inches). Always insert the spade vertically; this ensures a consistent depth of dig.

Move backwards and dig another trench, turning the soil from that trench into the previous empty trench. At the end of the row, turn the soil from the row by your side and work your way back to where you have piled the soil from the first trench that you will use to fill the final trench.

Alternatively, you can barrow the soil from the first trench to the end of a row to fill the last trench but this adds an unnecessary amount of work to the job.

Leave the soil in clods; the action of winter frosts will break them down for you so that in spring you can easily obtain a fine tilth.

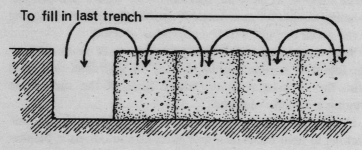

To fill in last trench

Fig. 1. Single digging.

Double Digging
Double digging is a more thorough method where the bottom of the trench is broken up with a fork to another spit's depth before the soil from the next trench is added. Usually some compost or manure is laid on the forked over soil before being covered. This feeds and thereby encourages the worms to break down and mix the soil to a greater depth, increasing the growing depth of your soil.

If your topsoil is thin, be careful not to mix the subsoil from the lower spit with the upper good soil as it will have a detrimental effect. The breaking up of the lower level combined with manure or compost will, over the years, produce a topsoil some 50cm (20 inches) deep and perfect for all crops.

Double digging should always be done when breaking new or neglected ground; thereafter, depending on your soil, every three to five years will be sufficient.

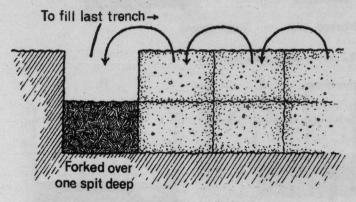

Fig. 2. Double digging.
This consists of turning over the first spit and breaking up the second spit.

Full Trenching

Full trenching is rarely done nowadays except by the keenest of growers or those needing to break up a low hard pan to improve drainage. It requires a good depth of topsoil already there to be effective, between 30cm and 45cm (12 and 18 inches) at a minimum.

A double width trench is dug, the soil being reserved for the final infill. A trench is taken from half the width and this soil also reserved. A third spit down is then forked over, organic matter added and the soil from the other half of the trench moved over it.

Next, a third trench is started, with the soil being placed on top of the first and so forth to the end. It is hard to explain but quite simple in practice as the diagram overleaf shows.

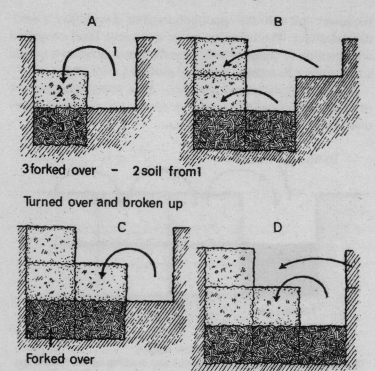

Fig. 3. Trenching.
This is an extension of double digging to include a third level of soil.

The No-Digging Method

This theory has been around for many years and appeals to gardeners as on the surface it offers an easier method of cultivation.

Each year a layer of organic matter (compost and manure) at least 7.5cm (3 inches) and preferably 10cm (4 inches) deep is laid onto the surface of the soil and left to the worms to take down to the lower levels.

The first drawback is that of obtaining this amount of organic matter. For an ordinary allotment of 250 square metres you would require some 25 cubic metres each year. This is a huge amount, equivalent to two large skip loads and well beyond the compost produced from that plot. Actually moving that amount of organic matter is probably more work than digging over anyway.

Nevertheless, a proper study of this method was carried out in the 1970s by the Henry Doubleday Research Association (now called Garden Organic). In the early years of the experiment an increase in productivity was observed over a conventionally managed plot. However, after a few years the productivity crashed as the soil below became panned.

This leads me to the conclusion that if your soil is in good condition you need not dig over each year but you do need to dig over on occasion to maintain fertility. The exception to this rule would be a clay soil. In my experience these should be dug over every year if possible because they very quickly revert from a good condition and benefit from the winter freeze.

Drainage

Waterlogged soil, where the water stays unmoved for days, will not grow good vegetables. Growth and development are checked and in extreme cases plants will drown. Roots actually require some air to be available to thrive which is why you can drown them. Aquatic plants have evolved in different conditions from those in which our vegetables flourish.

In these days of climate change where we do not know if summer will bring drought or flood, good drainage is more important than ever for good production.

How to Test for a Water Level

To check how your plot drains and if you suffer waterlogging you should test. At the lowest part of the plot dig a hole about 60cm (2 feet) square and 75cm (30 inches) deep. A week after heavy rain take a look at the hole to see what water is in there. If the water fills around half the hole or more, then drainage is required. If just a few centimetres of water lie on the bottom, then you will get away with just double digging.

Raised Beds

If you have poor drainage and a high water table then consider raised deep beds where the plants are lifted above the water. If need be, you can make the beds higher than normal but, in any case, the paths will be wet and tend to become muddy so a thick layer of gravel on them will be needed to keep the mud off your boots.

How to Drain

There are two excellent methods, one using pipes and the other brushwood or stones.

A satisfactory depth of drain should be 50–60cm (20–24 inches) with the drains spaced from 2–3 metres (6½–10 feet) apart.

It is well worth investing in a specific drain spade, which has a long narrow blade designed just for this task. They are available quite cheaply (less than £15) and will halve the time the job takes.

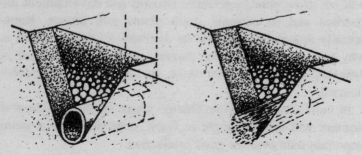

Fig. 4. Drainage: (left) with pipes; (right) with brushwood.

The drain trenches should be around 60cm (24 inches) deep and 2–3 metres (6½–10 feet) apart, ideally in a herringbone pattern over the area, side trenches running into the central trench and with a slope towards the lowest point, since water has yet to be made to run uphill!

A shallow layer of clinker or coarse gravel is placed in the base of the trench and then the perforated plastic pipes are laid in. Check with a spirit level that the pipe has a slope at frequent intervals and adjust if required. More coarse gravel is then poured over the pipe and to the sides with finer gravel above this before the soil is replaced.

If pipes are too expensive, the bottom of the trench should be filled up to 30cm (12 inches) or so with large stones or clinkers, or with a 20cm (8 inch) layer of brushwood, preferably of oak or ash, pressed down by trampling with the feet. Pipes are a more permanent solution but brushwood should last a good few years. It's a good idea to make and keep a plan of your drains so in years to come you will know their location if a blockage occurs. See Fig 4.

You need to lead the water away so, if there is a ditch handy, lead the pipes to end there. If there is no opportunity to lead the water away, then you will need to dig a soakaway in the lowest part of the plot. This is a large hole, around 2 metres (6½ feet) wide and around the same depth filled with rubble, stones and clinker and the top 60cm (24 inches) of soil replaced on top as a growing area. This is a large job and you may find it better to employ a builder with a mini-digger to do it for you in a couple of hours.

Fig. 5. A soakaway.
A deep hole is dug at the lowest convenient point,
and filled up with rubble or large stones.

3

PLANNING THE GARDENING YEAR

The Garden Diary

One of the most useful things for any gardener is a diary. Unless you are blessed with perfect recall, it will prove invaluable for you as the years pass. In the diary you keep a record of your plans, your actions, the conditions and the results. It need not be well written or overly detailed but it must be written up regularly or you will forget what you did.

Record what you sow, including the variety and the date and where you have sown. Make a note of what the weather is like, especially frosts because we all have our own micro climate and knowing when the first and last frosts are likely to occur is very useful. It's also good to record what the eventual harvest is like both in quantity and acceptability.

When you come to order your seeds, a review of your diary will remind you that variety X worked well whereas variety Y was a failure. What grows well for you may not be the same as what grows well for a grower with different soil and weather conditions. It is easy to become confused regarding what was planted where; again your diary will ensure you keep track.

To remind yourself when jobs need doing, put a brief note

in your forthcoming diary, such as 'sow lettuce Tom Thumb', on the relevant date, and tick off when you've carried out the task.

What to Grow

One of the silliest things I often come across is the grower who has a crop that he or she doesn't like and that the family loathe. So the first rule is to grow what you like and want to eat. Although this may seem obvious, in my experience it is often strangely ignored.

On the other hand, do try new crops that you may not have eaten before. The worst case is that you waste a packet of seeds and a little land. Having made a list of what you eventually want to eat, choose the varieties you want to grow.

Buying Seeds

I strongly recommend you contact three or four reputable seed suppliers before making your selection. I say reputable because not all seed suppliers' quality is the highest. Beginners may sow a packet of seeds and when none comes up they assume it is their method at fault whereas the truth may be that the germination rate of the seeds is appalling. Seeds stored incorrectly or old seeds may just simply be dead. If you buy a pack of seeds from a reputable supplier and none germinates, return the packet and unused seeds left in there with a letter of explanation. The supplier will compensate you if the seeds are at fault; and your action also assists them in maintaining standards

It is always a temptation to go for the lowest price but this can often be false economy. Seeds, even within their 'shelf life' reduced to clear in a store at the end of the season may well have been subject to poor storage and be dead in the packet.

Settle yourself down with your list of what you want and carefully read through the catalogues.

Take into account where you are growing; container

growers and raised bed growers should look for varieties
suitable for close spacing or what are sometimes described as
mini-veg.

Royal Horticultural Society Award of Garden Merit
Some varieties have won the Royal Horticultural Society
Award of Garden Merit. This means that they have been
evaluated by independent experts for their suitability for the
ordinary gardener to obtain good results. This will be flagged
up by the supplier and is a reliable guideline to follow.

You will find that these varieties are more tolerant of
mistakes in cultivation and poor conditions than standard
varieties and that they often crop over a longer period than
standard varieties. Often seeds are developed for use by the
farmer and, in very controlled conditions, are extremely
productive cropping in a short period but this is not what you
require. You are looking at flavour, long cropping periods and
tolerance or disease resistance.

If you have that curse of the cabbage family, club-root
(see page 113), in your soil you will be happy to know that
you can now buy varieties that are resistant to it. This does
not mean they are immune but that you are far more likely
to succeed in producing a crop where a standard variety
would fail utterly.

Heritage or Heirloom Varieties
You might like to consider buying a few 'heritage' varieties to
try. These are just old varieties, often near a hundred years old.
Seed suppliers spend a fortune on developing new varieties,
breeding for characteristics that will improve sales over their
rivals in the market place. Unfortunately for the home grower,
the big bucks are in seeds that will be popular with farmers
and professional growers rather than us. This means that the
ability to hold on in the ground until you are ready to harvest
or crop over a period is not high on the list, neither is taste
although the supermarkets are now catching on to increased

sophistication in their customers who want to buy vegetables that taste as good as they look.

The heritage variety may well offer exceptional taste but do not put all your eggs into one basket: grow them alongside a modern variety. One hundred years of breeding has often resulted in a far superior plant.

The Garden Organic association operates The Heritage Seed Library which aims to conserve and make available vegetable varieties that are not widely available or have been de-listed thanks to EU rules that came into effect in 1978 to control the market. The cost of listing under those rules, assuming you could get your seed listed, was prohibitive for the suppliers and reduced dramatically the range available to the home grower.

F1 Hybrids
You will notice that some seeds are described as F1 hybrids. What this means is that they are the first generation result of crossing two different varieties. This often results in something called hybrid vigour where the hybrid grows really strongly and produces a better crop than either of its parents.

Unfortunately you cannot save seeds from F1 hybrids; they will not be true to the parent and the results are very unpredictable.

Sorting and Storing Your Seeds
When your seeds arrive, sort them into sowing order (earliest first) and store in a cool dark place. Don't forget that growing instructions in a book are of necessity standardized so check the seed packet, especially for those close-spaced varieties.

One crop I prefer to buy from a garden centre than from mail order are seed potatoes. Once more, choose your varieties carefully and then ask your store if they will be stocking or can obtain those for you. This way you can confirm quality before you buy.

Planning Your Plot

Whatever methods you are using to grow in (raised beds, containers or a patch of land), you need to think what should go where. First, consider any permanent plantings. A comfrey patch remains from year to year as does an asparagus bed or rhubarb planting. Once these are settled, you can plan your rotation.

Crop Rotation

For container growers, rotation is irrelevant. The compost is changed annually so in effect everything is rotated but for other growers rotation is vital.

The simplest rule of rotation is not to grow the same thing in the same place year after year. Growing the same crop in the same place will result in a build-up of pests and disease specific to that crop. Different crops use different levels of nutrients so eventually the nutrients get out of balance, some depleted but others in excess. Some gardeners persist in growing their runner beans or onions in the same place each year but it has been proven this is not a good idea – not every old fashioned method is good!

There are many different systems for rotating crops, some fairly crude and some quite complex, designed to ensure that the following crops utilize nutrients left by the previous crops. The simplest method, a three-year rotation, runs like this:

	Year 1	Year 2	Year 3
Plot 1	Potatoes	Brassicas	Everything Else
Plot 2	Brassicas	Everything Else	Potatoes
Plot 3	Everything Else	Potatoes	Brassicas

In the winter preceding Year 1 manure is added to Plot 1 for the potatoes, who also prefer their soil somewhat acid, and lime is added to Plot 2 for the brassicas who like their soil neutral. In Year 2 you manure Plot 3 and lime Plot 1.

This basic system does work to some degree but you are unlikely to find your crops actually fit in so precisely.

A four- or even five-year rotation is more effective at preventing a build-up of problems. My preferred method is as follows:

In the first year following manure, I grow the potatoes. I usually follow these with mustard as a green manure which also prevents the eelworm from arriving in season and thereby reduces the population.

A good dose of lime is applied to take the pH up to around 6 in the winter and the next year peas and beans are sown. These share an amazing ability. On their roots are nodules which contain bacteria that fix nitrogen from the air – thereby feeding the crop and providing nutrients for the following crop.

Next on the rotation are the brassicas. These all like a well limed soil so I check the pH and lime after the peas and beans around the planting area if necessary to take the pH back up.

The next year the root crops have their turn: carrots, parsnips, salsify and scorzonera.

The last year the onion family is grown (onions, garlic and leeks), followed by a good load of manure for the potatoes the next year.

Everything else is fitted in as we go along. Sweetcorn, for example, likes a lot of nitrogen so these go early in the plan, usually alongside the pea family with some additional nitrogen. Squashes and pumpkins are grown in the space beside the root crops.

Potatoes and brassicas take up the most room so they rarely share the bed with anything else.

It is not an exact science but the important thing is to avoid repetition, planting crops in the same family in the same place year on year. You will grow what you like in the quantities that suit you and will learn the best way to rotate for yourself. This is one of the joys of growing your own, experimenting and altering over time as everything changes.

Crop Families

It is helpful when planning your rotation to know what vegetable belongs in what family for they are likely to share the same likes and dislikes as well as being susceptible to the same problems.

These main groups are:

Solanaceae – the potato family, which also includes tomatoes and aubergines.

Cruciferae – the cabbage tribe, formerly known as *Brassicaceae* from which we get brassica. This includes all the cabbages, cauliflowers, kale and (this may surprise you) turnips, radishes and swedes as well as landcress and mustard.

Umbelliferae – this includes carrots, parsnips, Hamburg and ordinary parsley, celery and celeriac.

Liliaceae – the lily family of which alliums (*allium* is Latin for garlic) are a subset. This includes onions, shallots and leeks.

Leguminosae – the bean family of legumes. Anything with 'bean' in the name (runner, French, broad, field) and peas which are one of the oldest food crops grown by man.

Cucurbitaceae – the cucurbit family includes cucumbers, marrows, courgettes and pumpkins as well as cucumbers.

Species not listed above, like sweetcorn, can be considered out of the family groups and safely intermixed with them. Salsify and scorzonera are members of the *Compositae* family but best considered as *Umbelliferae* along with the parsnips.

4

GETTING THE MOST FROM YOUR LAND

Most vegetable growers wish for more land at some point but land is finite so how can you produce more from less?

Keep the Land Working for You
Vacant land, that is land without a crop on it, will outside of winter happily produce a crop of weeds so keeping it working will not only benefit you in higher yields but also in less pointless work weeding vacant land.

After the early potatoes are harvested in June/July, the vacant land can be sown with a green manure to benefit the soil or you could sow French beans, which provide their own nitrogen and are tolerant of a lower pH than the ideal, lettuce or fast growing turnips, even runner beans started in pots. This may seem to run contrary to the rotation plan but as long as you avoid the same thing year after year it will make little difference.

Intercropping is another way to maximize production. It is important to observe recommended spacing between plants. These distances have been calculated to produce the most from a given area and adjusted by the seed supplier to suit the individual variety. Overcrowding will not produce more from the space but you can share the space between rows of slow growing crops with fast growing crops that will be ready before being shaded out. Early carrots, such as Nantes varieties, or turnips will be ready in 8–10 weeks from sowing so allowing time for them to have developed before the broad beans have covered them.

Successional Sowing and Starting in Pots

It is easy to freeze vegetables and store your surplus but fresh vegetables, especially really fresh vegetables picked a few hours earlier, taste best. So to avoid growing a glut through the season, we need to have smaller quantities of the same crop ripening over a period.

Let's say we're going to use a cauliflower each week. Take a modular seed tray, fill with compost and sow 3 cells, label with the variety and date. Three weeks later sow another 3 cells and so forth. As the plants develop, pot on into 8cm (3 inch) pots and when ready into the ground. This way you are producing a continuous supply for the table rather than a dozen cauliflowers in one go.

Obviously this method can be applied to any crop that can be started in pots. It is especially useful for lettuces, which tend to bolt if left too long anyway. Bolting is where the plant attempts to produce seed as it thinks it is at the end of its life. This results in tall stems rather than edible leaves. The other benefit of this method is that the land is in use for less time, since the crop has been grown in pots to the point of needing the space in the ground.

Extend the Season

The British summer has always been a gamble for the gardener, in fact it is often said that we do not have a climate but we do have weather. April can bring snow one year and summer sunshine the next, all of which hardly helps us. By protecting our crops we can extend our season at both ends, bringing the land into use earlier and for longer.

Horticultural Fleece

For large areas horticultural fleece is an excellent investment. It creates a micro climate just a degree or two higher at ground level, but this is enough to make the difference between a frosted dead plant and a live productive plant.

As the plants grow, if sufficient slack has been allowed, the fleece will rise on top of the foliage, keeping the crop protected. By laying the fleece a week or two before sowing the soil can be pre-warmed a little, helping the crop to get off to a good start. First early potatoes are one crop that will really benefit from the use of fleece since an unexpected frost will, at best, check growth. Fleece can be wrapped around a runner bean wigwam should a late frost threaten them.

Good quality fleece will last a number of years if it is stored dry when not in use. It is common to hold the fleece in place by means of pegs driven through into the ground but this damages the fleece, reducing its useful lifespan. A better method of holding fleece in place is to fill 2-litre plastic milk containers with water, or preferably sand which doesn't tend to leak, and use these 'soft bricks' to weigh the edges down. Real house bricks tend to tear the fleece.

Cloches

The first cloches were glass bell jars or lantern cloches made with panes of glass in a frame which were placed over the plants. These are still available but more for their decorative value nowadays since they are very expensive.

The next cloche system to become popular was simple panes of horticultural glass, usually around 30cm x 60cm (12 x 24 inches) leaning against each other to form a tent and held by a clip at the top. These were placed in rows with another pane used to close off the end to prevent a wind tunnel effect.

More sophisticated was the barn cloche where two panes were used as vertical sides with two smaller panes to form a tent above, all held together with a complex frame and clip of metal.

Although both of these are excellent and effective they have some drawbacks in that glass is expensive and fragile. There is also the risk of injury when handling and working near glass to consider – certainly not a system to use in a garden where children are about.

Nowadays low cost, plastic tubular cloches are available which are far easier to erect since they incorporate pegs by design. Made from heavy gauge polythene, they are still lightweight and fold down for storage in the shed when not in use. They still require the open ends to be closed off when not in use and a piece of glass or, a safer option, a piece of rigid clear plastic will do the job. Because they are so lightweight, they can be blown off and damaged in strong winds. On windy sites, bamboo poles driven in by the sides and angled over the cloches will hold them down.

Because the plastic degrades in sunlight, to maximize their life they should be taken down and stored away when not in use.

There are variations on the theme, including tunnel cloches made from very thin polythene which often do not last the season, being too easily torn. Once again, quality pays. Solid tunnel cloches made from corrugated plastic and in smooth clear versions are available and these are satisfactory.

Cloches are a very worthwhile investment, not only keeping crops safe that would otherwise be killed by frost but bringing on growth in the warmer environment within.

Hot Beds

I mention these since I am often asked about them but I do not think they are worthwhile for the modern gardener whose time is valuable and can afford easier solutions.

They were developed at the end of the nineteenth century by head gardeners who had to provide high quality crops for their masters in 'the big house' out of season. The head gardener would delegate the work to his extensive staff, of course!

A brick-built large coldframe was filled with fresh horse or cow manure and covered with a layer of fine sieved soil. After a few weeks the temperature would stabilize and the decomposing manure provide bottom heat for the crops above under glass.

Rather than expend the time and energy of loading and eventually unloading some two or three cubic metres of manure, modern gardeners can use an electrically heated bench in a greenhouse.

Coldframes

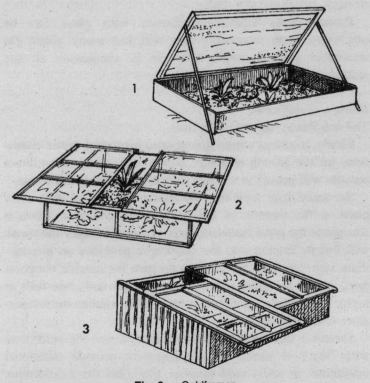

Fig. 6.   Coldframes.
(1) Wooden box frame with polythene lid.
(2) Purpose-made aluminium and glass coldframe.
(3) Home-made frame.

These vary in size but are generally around 1.2 metres (4 feet) long by 50–60cm (20–24 inches) wide and around 40–50cm (16–20 inches) high at the rear, sloping down to the front. They can have glass sides and top or solid sides with a glass top.

All glass coldframes obviously allow more light in but solid sides can be a little warmer. Solid sided coldframes can be easily built by anyone with moderate carpentry skills, the lights often being recycled widow lights. It is well worth keeping an eye out for double glazing installations and just asking. An effective light can be constructed by fixing a sheet of thick polythene to a frame.

Purpose-made aluminium frames with glass can be purchased quite reasonably and will last many years. Do remember glass is fragile and can be dangerous, so site suitably.

Using a Coldframe
The coldframe has two main uses:

Firstly, it acts as a mini greenhouse providing better conditions for the growth of plants. Seeds that can be sown direct outside will get off to a better start in modules in the frame.

Secondly, it is used for 'hardening off'. If we start off a plant in the warmth of the greenhouse and then move it straight to the great outdoors, there is a good chance the shock will kill it. Placing into the coldframe provides an intermediate step, allowing the plant to prepare for outside temperatures. Leave the lights open on a warm day and close fully at night. It is a crude but effective method to regulate the temperature inside the frame.

Should a sudden hard frost threaten, cover the coldframe with fleece or sheets of newspaper to provide additional insulation. In really cold weather, the solid sided coldframe excels due to it being warmer.

5

WEEDS AND WHAT TO DO ABOUT THEM

There is an old saying that *'one year's seeding is seven years' weeding'* and unfortunately this is not true. Some weeds can wait their chance to spring into life for far longer than seven years.

Most annual weeds spread thousands of seeds that lie in the ground until conditions are right and then appear. Turning over the soil brings those seeds from yesteryear to the surface and up they pop.

Luckily, most of these annual weeds are pretty easy to deal with. Just hoe through them, leave them to dry on the surface and then collect them for the compost heap. Catching them young is most effective – better to hoe little and often. A sharp Dutch hoe is a joy to use, just angle it so that the blade is horizontal to the surface and move the hoe back and forth, just under the soil surface. This slices the weed off its root and both root and stem die.

Do not hoe in wet weather though, the soil clings onto the hoe and you end up pushing the weeds from the ground rather than cutting them. Worse still, they probably survive and re-root.

There are other weeds that present a bigger challenge. These are perennial and live from year to year, As a general rule, hoeing them just cuts the top off and they pop back from their deep roots – it seems with more vigour as well!

For some weeds the only method (realistically) is chemical sprays but where possible try non-chemical methods.

The main perennial weeds you will find are:

Nettles

Nettles form a mass of yellowish roots, from which they happily re-grow. Nettles tend to be full of goodness (yes you can eat young ones) both for us and the garden. Taking frequent cuts with shears or scythe will, eventually, kill the plant off. If you have a patch of nettles in a corner, use them as a compost mine. Otherwise, dig out the roots and watch out for re-growth from the small pieces you are bound to miss.

Fig. 7. Nettle.

Nettles seem to prefer an acid soil, and liming to a pH above 5.5 or 6.0 seems really to slow them down.

Dock Leaves

Where there are nettles, you will find docks. They have a long tap root from which they will re-grow. You have to dig out the root and then kill it. You can either leave the root to dry out or drown it in a barrel of water to do this.

Be careful about rotavating where there are docks – the root cuttings will all leap up, multiplying your problem many fold.

Fig. 8.   Dock leaves.

Dandelions

Like docks, they have a deep root but are not quite so
vigorous. Treat as docks.

And, yes, you can eat them as a salad if you're really
hungry.

Fig. 9.   Dandelion.

Bindweed

Bindweed (*Convolvulus*) is quite pretty with its trumpet-
shaped white flowers. It grows about a foot a second when
your back is turned, strangling any crops you have planted.

Under the soil it produces white running roots, which travel along popping up when you think you have got it all.

Fig. 10. Bindweed.

Basically dig out the roots; even a piece an inch long is enough to start it off. Small infestations can be coped with by hand but if you have a serious amount then you probably need to go chemical.

Glyphosate will kill it off but it may require a couple of applications. You can either spray it or paint it directly onto the leaves. Allowing the leaves to climb up a frame and then spraying to try to maximize the amount of poison getting to the roots is effective when dealing with a serious infestation.

Couch or Twitch Grass

Couch grass (twitch) is another plant with creeping underground stems. Treat as you would bindweed. The roots are smaller than bindweed roots, which makes them harder to find and remove. It grows away from bits of root as small as 2cm (1 inch) so rotavation is a great way to spread it.

Couch grass is very susceptible to shading so you can kill it by covering with old carpet, black plastic, etc., for a couple of months. Ordinary grass is far easier to deal with, just treat as lawn grass, cutting a few centimetres below the surface and stacking upside down until it turns to loam. You will know the difference by the root system: couch has spreading white tubes where ordinary grass roots are small and fibrous.

Fig. 11. Couch or twitch grass.

Horsetail or Mare's Tail

Horsetail or mare's tail, *Equisetum arvense*, is, in my opinion, public enemy number one. It looks like it belongs in Jurassic Park and, unchecked, spreads like wildfire.

In spring, brown green shoots appear with small cones at the tips that produce spores, and it grows away from creeping thin brown roots that you can hardly see as they are soil coloured. Digging out these roots is not feasible – they go down into the soil for up to 1.5 metres (5 feet).

Fig. 12. Horsetail or mare's tail.

Later the 'leaves' or tails appear. These will die off as autumn turns to winter and the roots sit there waiting for spring. The leaves have a waxy coat, which makes the plant highly resistant to weedkillers.

Crushing the leaves to break up the coating helps weedkiller to penetrate and become absorbed but in large areas it is not so easy to crush all the leaves. However, glyphosate weedkiller will have an effect and eventually kill the plant. You may even need five or more applications. Knock it back, it re-grows and you repeat the process. Because you need to repeat the applications, the ground will be out of action for a whole season, unfortunately.

I've been told that horsetail can be eradicated organically by digging through the soil and removing the roots followed by hoeing off a few centimetres below the surface as shoots appear but I have not seen it work in practice.

Even after chemical treatment, it still comes up from isolated pieces of root. These can be dealt with by digging out, as long as action is taken as soon as they are noticed and before those roots can really develop.

Until recently, you could use a weedkiller called ammonium sulphamate which is chemically similar to sulphate of ammonia, a nitrogen fertilizer, but does not provide nutrition to the plant. Indeed it acts like carbon monoxide in our bloodstream does, replacing and blocking the uptake of oxygen, but in this case it is blocking nitrogen.

After six to eight weeks the ammonium sulphamate transformed to sulphate of ammonia and it was perfectly safe to plant out. Unfortunately the cost of the EU approval process was too much for the manufacturers and so this effective and safe product is not in our armoury, thanks to the bureaucrats.

Glyphosate

This herbicide is said to be very safe. It is systemic, being taken down to the roots and is deactivated by contact with the soil. It is not approved by UK organic standards but is often the lesser of two evils when faced with a large plot of land covered with perennial weeds. It is the main constituent in Round Up and Tumbleweed ready mixed.

It is quite economical but don't use that as an excuse to over use it. The dead weeds can be composted without the compost becoming toxic. Weedkillers should always be treated with caution.

6

TOOLS

When people start gardening and growing their own vegetables, one of the first things that they think about is equipment. There is a bewildering array of tools and tool systems you can buy, ranging from the basic humble spade to exotically named mattocks and azadas.

In fact, you don't actually need that much in the way of tools and, although there are many different and useful tools out there, it's best to concentrate on buying good quality basic tools to start with and leave the fancy tools until you are sure about what you want.

A well made tool will last longer than a lifetime, so before rushing out to the shops check your local paper for second-hand tools or offer to buy tools from elderly gardeners who are giving up.

The Spade
The first tool that I think you must have is a digging spade. It will double as a shovel as well. The shovel is generally just used to move earth and so forth but the digging spade is for, well, digging.

You can buy stainless steel spades, which do tend to slip through clay soils easily but an ordinary spade still does the job. Most important is to get the handle height right. People are taller nowadays than they used to be and a longer handle makes the spade easier to use for them and gives better leverage.

At the risk of being called sexist, ladies should consider a border spade which has a smaller blade. It's a lot easier to use if you don't have the strength to handle a full sized spade with a chunk of soil on the blade. When I was digging a trench through very solid clay, I found that the border spade enabled me to complete the job where the full size spade was just too hard to handle.

Some spades are turned at the top of the blade to provide a flat surface to press on which I would recommend if you have a heavy soil as the sharp topped spade wears your boots and the pressure can become uncomfortable.

Before buying, check that the height is comfortable, the blade and shaft sound and that they are firmly fixed to each other. Handles come in two types, the basic 'T' handle and the 'D' or 'Y' handle. The 'D' style is preferred by many gardeners but it is what you find comfortable that matters. (See Fig. 13 overleaf.)

The Shovel

A shovel is a spade where the sides and top are upturned to form a container and prevent spillage. They are used for moving quantities of loose material like sand or gravel and not for digging. Whilst you can use a spade as a shovel (the extra material held by the shovel shortens the task of moving a pile of sand, for example), you cannot use a shovel as a digging spade.

The Fork

Some gardeners would argue that the fork is more important than the spade but either way the same rules apply. It must be strong and of the right size for you as well as the job. It is critical that the tines are strong. If you can bend them, then in short order they will be bent by stones in the ground and eventually useless. The smaller border fork is useful when working in close confines even if you can handle the full size fork.

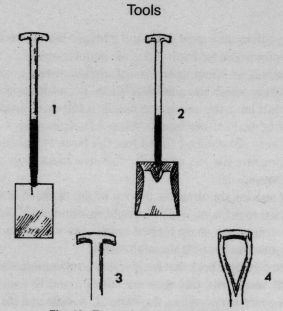

Fig. 13. Types of spades and handles.
(1) Digging spade.   (2) Shovel with wide blade and raised edges.
(3) 'T' handle.   (4) 'D' or 'Y' handle.

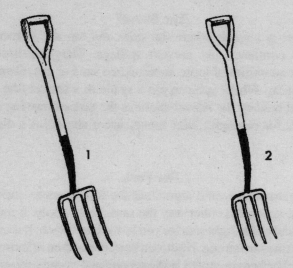

Fig. 14. Forks.
(1) Digging fork.
(2) Border or 'ladies' fork.

One variant on the fork is the potato fork. This has flat rather than square section blades and is designed to go into the soil easily and lift potatoes that will not fall through the reduced space between the tines. I have a potato fork and quite frankly am not convinced it is worth the room in the shed.

The Rake

This is necessary to level soil surfaces, rake down lumps, remove stones, clear off rubbish and, in some cases, draw out drills. Once again, a strong construction with a reasonable shaft is essential.

As well as the garden rake, there is also a spring tine or sprung rake which you use for de-thatching lawns and clearing mowings. Usually this doesn't have a job on the vegetable patch.

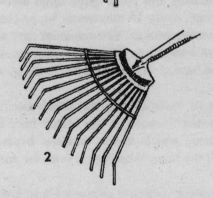

Fig. 15. Rakes.
(1) Garden rake.
(2) Sprung rake.

The Hoe

The hoe is probably the most used tool on a vegetable plot. It is used to cut down weeds, loosen the soil and give a preliminary thinning to crowded crops.

There are a number of different types of hoe available but I think a Dutch hoe and a draw hoe are all you really need, apart from an additional tool that you must have with a hoe – a sharpening implement. This can be a small sharpening stone or, as I use, a metal file that I use to keep an edge on the blade. A sharp hoe is a joy to use but a blunt hoe is hard work.

The draw hoe is used by pulling it towards you, chopping into the weeds, and it is very useful for drawing a drill whether for sowing seeds or deeper for planting potatoes.

The Dutch hoe is used by pushing the blade just under the soil surface, thereby cutting the weeds away from their roots. You need to hold the hoe so that the blade is level to the ground or it will dig in or plane over the weeds. A back and forth motion is ideal and, with practice, you can control positioning very accurately and cover quite large areas in a short time. Usually I stop every 15 minutes or so, just to give the blade a few sharpening strokes. You can work forwards if cutting larger weeds or backwards if hoeing seedlings so that you can see where you have covered and avoid walking on the hoed plot.

There are a couple of variations on the Dutch hoe: a flat weeding push hoe, which is used as the Dutch hoe; and a push-pull weeding hoe, which has a serrated blade that remains in the soil all the time, working on both the forward and back strokes.

Finally, there is the Swoe, which is an angled head hoe with three cutting edges. The Swoe is one of those tools that are not popular, due to their strange shape perhaps, but many owners swear by it. If you can, try one out to see if it suits you.

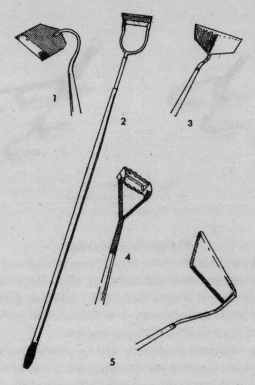

Fig. 16. Hoes.
(1) Draw hoe.
(2) Dutch hoe with plastic grip.
(3) Flat weeding push hoe.
(4) Push-pull weeding hoe.
(5) Swoe.

Hand Cultivator

This is a tool which loosens, aerates and breaks up most types of light soil quickly and thoroughly with ease. It is not so useful on heavy clay soils. Usually it has three tines but you can get five-tined models.

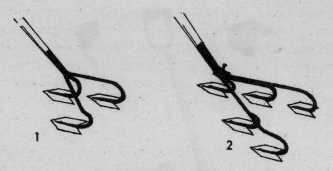

Fig. 17. Cultivators.
(1) Three-prong cultivator.
(2) Five-prong cultivator.

Mattocks or Azadas

A mattock, sometimes know by its Spanish name of Azada, is a broad blade on a stout handle rather like a larger scale draw hoe. For digging it is used more like a pickaxe than a spade, lifting the blade and allowing it to fall into the soil. It is also used like a draw hoe for clearing ground.

It is the standard gardening tool in many countries from South America to Spain and Portugal and is one of those tools that some users love and swear by whereas others find it no benefit over the usual tools available in the UK. Try before you buy.

Hand Tools

Just as with your full tools, it is important to get quality hand tools. That bargain trowel for 50p or a pound probably won't last you a month.

There are four hand tools that are really useful:

A **hand trowel** for digging holes – your miniature spade. You can also get very narrow trowels which are great when working between close-planted crops.

A **hand fork** for loosening and breaking up the soil just like its larger version.

An **onion hoe** for weeding close to plants and in raised beds is very useful as well, although these are becoming harder to find.

Finally, a **double hoe** where one side is a blade for hoeing and drawing drills, with three tines on the other side for cultivating.

Wolf manufacture an inter-changeable range of tool heads that can be attached to different handles, enabling you to use a cultivator as both a hand tool and as a full tool. If you have a combination of raised beds and normal soil, these can be an economical solution to buying quality tools.

Special hand tools such as the Easi-Grip range are also available for those with mobility problems, due to arthritis, etc. The handle is at 90 degrees to the tool, enabling the force line to pass in a straight line through the wrist and arm.

There are also full sized tools such as the Lite Lift range designed for older gardeners or those suffering from back, neck or arm problems. They're very light – you can balance them on one finger – and ergonomically shaped and with an additional handle that can be positioned for optimum control.

Fig. 18. Wolf interchangeable cultivator head.

Shears and Secateurs

For green manure crops like mustard, shears are invaluable for cutting them down. Like a hoe, keep them sharp. You can use a file or a small sharpening stone for this. Secateurs are useful for small pruning jobs, clipping off a stalk when harvesting, etc.

Bow Saw and Loppers

If you have fruit trees to prune or overhanging trees and bushes, then a pair of long-handled lopping shears will be invaluable as will a bow saw. Unless you expect to use these frequently, just buy the least expensive models.

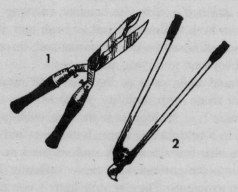

Fig. 19.   Shears.
(1) Hedge and all-purpose shears.
(2) Lopping shears.

Pegs and Line

Now this is one of the simplest tools but so useful I would call it essential. You can make your own with two sticks and a length of string, preferably the bright coloured nylon line you can find so you can always see it clearly. This gives a guide for digging and for drawing a row. Since the cost is negligible you may find it worthwhile having two or three lines.

Measuring Stick

This is a really simple aid to sowing and planting you make yourself for pennies. Take a length of 5cm x 2.5cm (2 inches x 1 inch) wood about 2 metres (6½ feet) long, and mark out, using an indelible marker or felt tip pen, on one side with a half width line every 15cm (6 inches) and a full width line every 30cm (12 inches). On the other side, mark similarly but with the half width lines every 10cm (4 inches). When sowing or planting, just lay the stick by the row and you have a spacing guide suitable for most plants.

Watering Can

You can buy a watering can very cheaply but you may find it worth spending more on a larger can to reduce walking back and forth to the tap or butt. Plastic cans are robust and light-weight, an important consideration since 10 litres of water weighs 10kg. Two cans are probably best, one in each hand halves the walking and balances the load.

Although the actual can is cheap to buy, you may need to spend more on the rose. This is the spray head and for watering seedlings you cannot beat a fine brass rose with its fine spray rather than one whose heavy flow knocks them down. When using a fine rose, turn it so it faces upwards and, when you tip the can, the water flows in a gentle arc, further reducing the force.

For the greenhouse you may want a smaller can, easier to handle when watering seed trays, etc., and a long-stemmed can is useful for getting water to crops at the back of a border.

Seed Trays and Modules

The standard seed tray is 36.5cm x 22cm x 5.5cm deep. This standardisation of the size is very useful because it enables a range of inserts to be used from different manufacturers.

It's worth paying extra for decent quality trays because the very thin trays may be cheap but they only last a year or two and have a nasty habit of collapsing when you pick them up, destroying the seedlings you've just grown!

You can just put compost into the tray and sow directly but with many plants it is preferable to avoid disturbing the roots and you will be better off sowing into modules. These are just plastic inserts placed into the seed tray that divide it up into cells so that the seedling can be taken out, with the compost, and either potted up or planted out without disturbing the roots.

The module inserts are available in a number of sizes, giving 12, 15, 24 or 40 cells per seed tray.

You can buy half-sized seed trays that are actually a little smaller than half size, enabling two to sit within a full-size tray. You can also get clear plastic propagator lids to sit on top of your seed tray. These provide a slightly warmer and more humid atmosphere to assist in germination.

You can make your own propagator by using some coat hanger wire to form a framework inserted into the corners of the tray and then insert the tray into a clear plastic bag.

Because some plants such as sweetcorn and beans really benefit from a deep tray you can use Rootrainers® modular cell system. These are deep modules with ridged sides that open up like a book to enable the plant to be removed with minimum root disturbance. The sides are ridged to guide the roots and prevent them from going round and round. They do work well but are quite expensive initially; however, they easily last for five years or more.

Pots

Traditionally, pots were made of clay and were expensive, fragile and, because of the porous material, prone to drying out. Nowadays, plastic is cheap, durable and impermeable. Pots are usually sized by either the diameter or volume. With plastic manufacture there is no reason for them to be round and square pots provide more volume for a given width and are easier to stack on the bench.

The most popular and useful size is the 3 inch (7.62cm) pot as most vegetables will go directly from this to their final planting position.

If you're on a tight budget, second-hand pots can often be picked up for free since garden centres sell many plants in pots. Washed they are perfectly serviceable. You can also use discarded plastic cups, such as those used by vending machines to deliver drinks. Heat the end of a meat skewer and use that to burn a few drainage holes into the base.

For large pots, useful for growing tomatoes, aubergines etc., some supermarkets and florists will sell or even give away the pots that cut flowers are delivered in. Drill some holes in the base and you have an expensive large pot for next to nothing.

Some Useful Accessories

Gloves – a decent pair of gardening gloves should be flexible enough to allow delicate movements of the fingers whilst providing protection from thorns, etc., as well as keeping your hands clean. If you like to work in the soil without gloves but wish to stop the soil becoming ingrained into your fingers then use some barrier hand cream before you commence work. This stops the skin wrinkling as it does if you soak in the bath for a long time and sucking the soil into your skin.

On the subject of working the soil with your hands, do ensure your tetanus vaccination is up to date. The tetanus bacterium (germ) lurks in the soil and especially manured soils, entering the body through a small cut or even the prick from a thorn, so all gardeners are at risk. It is quite rare in the UK because most people are vaccinated but it is a very serious disease that can be fatal.

Kneeling Pads and Stools – you will spend a lot of time on your knees, and pads that can be strapped to knees are available. A simple foam pad can be picked up for a few pounds that will save your knee joints and is well worth it. If getting up and down is difficult, then a kneeler stool or seat which provides an aid to getting back up is useful.

Wellingtons and Boots – sensible footwear not only keeps your feet clean and dry but provides protection. It's well worth paying for quality and you should really consider safety boots with extra protection if using a Rotavator.

Powered Machinery
Chippers and Shredders

Growing vegetables will produce a lot of green waste which should be turned into useful compost. A powered shredder will help tremendously in this. The smaller pieces produced by shredding have a greater surface area for the bacteria to act on and a compost pile made from shredded materials will heat up and rot down far faster than one made from unshredded material.

The larger the amount of waste you have, the larger machine you should buy since the throughput will be faster. In any case, a small shredder is better than no shredder.

The cheaper models are powered with electric motors but, if you do not have an electricity supply available, you can buy petrol engine powered models. The petrol engine shredders tend to be much more powerful and aimed at the professional market so unfortunately prices range upwards from five times that of electric models.

If you are working an allotment with no electricity, it is worth seeing if you can club together with other growers and buy a petrol shredder between you.

Rotavators and Tillers

For the larger garden, a Rotavator is a great investment. Although Rotavators may appear daunting at first sight, they are easy to use and will save many hours of hard work preparing the ground.

They are not a total substitute for digging (with a heavy clay soil even quite large Rotavators tend just to bounce over the surface), however they will break the soil up into a fine tilth in short order.

Just rotavating year after year will create a pan below the cultivation depth, so it is as well to dig over every three to five years in any case.

There is a wide range of machines available, ranging from small tillers to large walk-behind tractors so the choice can be bewildering. First, select a machine that you can handle. A machine with an engine size from 3hp to 6hp is suitable for most people and plots. Some of the larger machines have reverse gears, as well as more than one forward gear. These features make them easier to use than their size would suggest.

Consider the width of the tines. A narrow width enables you to manoeuvre better but a larger width covers more area in a pass. Most engines arc, nowadays, reliable and so the main thing to review is the quality of the tines. Weak tines that will bend or even break are to be avoided.

A Rotavator on an average vegetable plot will probably only run for 20 hours a year so an old second-hand machine can be worth buying. My own Merry Tiller is over 30 years old and starts every time, still performing as new. Unfortunately, the quality of new machines is rarely as good as that of the old ones.

Fig. 20. A mechanical cultivator.

Mantis Tillers

Unlike a full Rotavator that breaks up large areas of soil often to a depth of 30cm (12 inches) or more, a Mantis tiller is designed to produce a very fine tilth to a lesser depth, around 20cm–25cm (8–10 inches) maximum. They can even be used as a mechanical hoe, chopping the weeds as the soil is turned.

The Mantis is very lightweight (about 9kg/20 lb), with a tiller width of 22cm (nearly 9 inches), which makes it ideal for growers with raised beds as it can easily be lifted into and out of the bed.

Even if you have a full sized plot and a full sized Rotavator, a Mantis is worth considering additionally.

There are a wide range of accessories available, including a plough attachment, a furrow digging set of tines and accessories designed for lawn care such as a de-thatcher and border edger.

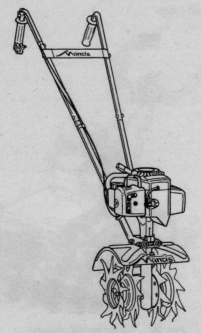

Fig. 21.   A Mantis tiller.

7

COMPOST, MANURES AND FERTILIZERS

The better your soil, the better the crops you will grow but to get that good soil you need to help it along. Many new growers fail to produce good crops because the foundation for their efforts – the soil – is poor.

Your soil consists of stones, rock dust and organic matter, which we call humus, which in turn holds the water, air and nutrition for your crops. If we can get those constituents right, then the soil will be right and we will be well rewarded for our labours.

Humus
As I said above, humus is the organic constituent of the soil. It comprises decayed vegetable and animal matter and is vital to the health of the soil.

It provides food for the millions of bacteria and thousands of worms that labour in a complex symbiosis to provide nutrients to the plant roots.

Humus lightens heavy clay soils allowing water to drain and roots to penetrate. It makes light sandy soils heavier, slowing the drainage and evaporation of water and holding nutrients for the crops.

Humus darkens the soil, which enables it to absorb

more solar energy and warm up faster and grow better crops.

There are four main ways we add humus to the soil: manures, green manures, leafmould and composts.

Manures

Manure is just animal dung, usually mixed with straw which has been allowed to age. Fresh manure is too strong to use on your plot and should be piled up and left for at least six and preferably twelve months before being utilized. This allows straw and bedding materials to rot down and mix, thereby 'calming' the manure. Cover the pile with a waterproof sheet to stop rain from washing nutrients out of the manure. Alternatively, fresh manure can be added to compost heaps to provide nitrogen which will activate the heap.

Different animal manures have different properties which I'll discuss below. Firstly, though, do not use dung from dogs or cats on your crops. This can contain disease and parasites that are harmful to us and their utilization is beyond the scope of this book.

The nutrient level in animal manures can vary wildly depending on the proportion of dung and urine to bedding materials, what those bedding materials are and how long the manure has been aged. However, they do provide a useful amount of nutrition as well as humus.

Horse and Cow Manure

Whether you live in country, town or city there is a good chance you will be able to get hold of horse manure. What to us gardeners is a valuable resource is a problematic waste product to many stables. On moving house, I telephoned the most local stable I could find in the book and asked if they had any manure. They were overjoyed to deliver a lorry load for free. Private horse owners often find themselves with a manure mountain that they are happy to give away. Even police stables have to dispose of the waste.

Horse manure works particularly well in clay soils, being

somewhat drier than cow manure but cow manure is far better than no manure. If you live in a farming area, it may well be that a local farmer will deliver a load of cow manure for a reasonable fee.

Because the nutritional analysis will vary between manures, there is no fixed rule for how much to apply. As a general rule, one barrow load per square metre applied every three years is a good rate to aim for. In a poor soil, lacking in humus, I would double that if possible.

Poultry Manure

Manure from chickens, turkeys or even pigeons can make a very useful contribution but is usually too strong to use directly on the land even when aged. The best way to make use of this resource is to add it to a compost heap; a layer about 1cm (½ inch) thick to a layer 15cm (6 inches) thick of green material will ensure the heap rots down quickly.

Rabbit and Guinea Pig Manure

Droppings and bedding materials from pet rabbits and guinea pigs are best just added to the compost heap as for poultry manure. There is not going to be enough to make it worthwhile directly applying to the land.

Sheep Manure

To obtain sheep manure you will probably have to collect it yourself with the permission of the landowner. It is unlikely that you would be asked to pay for it. Although it is a fair bit of work to collect it, sheep manure is excellent for making a liquid manure feed.

Green Manures

Green manures are plants which are grown to improve the structure and nutrient content of the soil. By growing green manure crops over winter, nutrients that would leach from the soil are held onto for the spring crops. Field beans and other legumes have the ability to fix nitrogen from the air making it available for the next crop.

Usually when ready the green manure is cut and allowed to wilt for a few days before being dug in to the soil. The plants decay and release nutrients as well as adding humus.

To overwinter, sow field beans, winter tares or Hungarian grazing rye. For early and mid season sowings, alfalfa, buckwheat, crimson clover or annual ryegrass are good options. After lifting potatoes, planting agricultural mustard will help to reduce eelworm by preventing them from breeding in season. Be careful though if you have club-root because mustard is a brassica which can further spread the disease.

The following table gives an overview of green manures:

Plant	Fixes Nitrogen	Sowing	Overwinters
Alfalfa	Yes	April–July	Yes
Field Beans	Yes	Sept–Nov	Yes
Buckwheat	No	April–Aug	No
Crimson Clover	Yes	April–Sept	No
Other Clovers	Yes	April–Aug	Yes
Fenugreek	No	March–Aug	No
Lupins	Yes	March–Jun	No
Mustard[1]	No	March–Sept	No
Fodder Radish[1]	No	Aug–Sept	No
Rye, Grazing	No	Aug–Sept	Yes
Rye, Annual Grass[2]	No	Spring or Autumn	Yes
Tares	Yes	March–Sept	Yes
Trefoil	Yes	March–Aug	Yes

1. Brassica which should be taken into account in rotation and especially if the plot is affected by club-root.
2. Annual Ryegrass does not bulk up as much as the traditional grazing rye but is easier to dig in.

Leafmould

Leafmould has negligible nutritional value but is useful as it adds humus and it can be used as an ingredient in potting composts. Making leafmould is very easy.

First collect autumn leaves. Sometimes road sweepers can be persuaded to donate a load to you.

Next construct a cage from wire netting. This can just be four posts driven into the soil with wire netting attached. Place the leaves in the container and leave for a year.

If you can only gather a small quantity of leaves, place them in a plastic bag pierced with ventilation holes, water them with a fine rose and place in a shady spot for a year. The process of decomposition will not be speeded up by adding anything, although if you have one of those marvellous garden vacuum mulchers that suck up leaves and chop them, you will find the leaves rot down much more quickly. Large quantities of leaves can be spread over a plot for the worms to draw down and dug over in the spring. This does tend to hold water and is best used on light sandy soils rather than heavy clay.

Compost

Making compost from garden waste is a relatively straight-forward process without any real mystery, although some old gardening books would have you believe that it was on a par with alchemy. On the other hand, you are turning lead into gold.

Compost Bins

First of all, you need two or preferably three compost bins. Nowadays you can get excellent plastic compost bins at subsidized rates from many local councils as well as pre-made decorative bins that would grace the finest garden, or you can build your own bin.

One easy method of constructing a compost bin is to find seven pallets and fix them together to form an 'M'. Two pallets form the back, two the sides and one the middle with the final two pallets forming 'doors' to hold the contents in. Since we want to hold heat in with the compost heap, stuff the insides of the pallets with cardboard as insulation.

You can, of course, build a more sophisticated version using treated timbers. Ideally, each bin should be between 90cm and 120cm square (3 and 4 feet square) and the same size high. There is nothing to stop you adding a third or even a fourth bin to the row if you wish.

Making Compost

First collect enough waste material together to start the heap. This waste can include any green waste from the garden with the exception of perennial weed roots which have a nasty habit of re-growing in the heap if it does not heat up properly. A good method to deal with these is to drown them under water for a few weeks until they start to rot and then they can be safely added to a heap.

Certain diseases can also be spread through the compost heap so avoid adding blighted potato haulm (potato foliage) or potatoes and brassica roots if you suffer with club-root. These should be disposed of as rubbish.

Most kitchen waste can and should be added to the heap but not meat or fish products or cooked pasta, etc., which will attract rats and flies. Do not add the contents of cat litter trays, dog droppings, etc., as these will create a significant health risk especially to children and pregnant women.

You can also add paper towels and bags, cardboard, cardboard tubes, egg boxes, wood chippings and small branches, old hay and straw and shredded paper. Be careful with lawn mowings if you have used a selective weedkiller on the lawn. Combined fertilizers like "Weed and Feed" contain a weedkiller that does not affect grass but harms other plants, like your crops, even after composting, so it is well worth checking before using lawn mowings in your compost.

Having collected your materials, it will help no end if you can put the material through a shredder, especially if using the hot method of making compost. Breaking thick stems down and shredding leaves into smaller pieces allows more surface area for the bacteria to work on. If you do not have a shredder, just try to cut larger items down into smaller pieces; brassica stems can be very woody and bashing with a lump hammer will help start the process.

You are looking to mix your waste so that things which do not rot quickly, like cardboard and twigs, are in with things that do, like lawn mowings or foliage. You are also looking to stop the compost from compressing which will exclude air and prevent decomposition.

Hot and Cold Heaps
The Cold Compost Heap
The easiest method is the 'cold' heap where you just add material to the bin as you go along, watering if necessary to keep the contents damp, but not soaking wet.

The addition of an activator will help speed rotting. This can be some fresh manure, a purpose-made compost activator – available in garden centres – or a small amount (25g) of sulphate of ammonia.

If you add this to a 15–20cm (6–8 inch) layer and then place another layer and dust with lime, this will help speed things along and keep the compost sweet. Do not directly mix the activator and the lime as it will cause an adverse reaction, stopping the activator from working properly

Eventually the materials will rot down, with compost at the bottom moving up to partially decomposed and fresh material at the top of the heap. The drawback of the cold heap method is that it does not heat up much and weed seeds can come through the process unharmed. It also takes a lot longer for compost to be made – sometimes as long as a year.

The Hot Compost Heap
This is more work but is far faster, as little as six weeks in summer, because the heap heats up and destroys weed seeds.

The resulting product is better as well, so this is the preferred method.

Collect enough material to fill a bin in one go and, as mentioned above, shred or cut up larger items. Place some woody material, sweetcorn stems, etc., in the bottom of the heap to allow some airflow into the base of the heap.

Put in a layer of between 15cm and 30cm (between 6 and 12 inches) of material and then add an activator, as mentioned above, followed by another layer of material, this time dusted with lime, and then add the next layer with an activator and so on until the bin is full. Ensure the material is damp, but not soaking wet, watering with a fine rose as you go.

Within a few days the heap should be warm or even hot to the touch, showing that those millions of bacteria are working hard for you. In a week or two, the heap will begin to cool down and this is the time to turn it.

The easiest way is to move it from one bin to the next or just take it out and throw it back in with a fork, checking that it is still damp and watering it if required. There is no need to add any more activator or lime after the first time.

The additional air and mixing from the edge to the centre may well cause the heap to heat up again, which is good. Repeat this process a few times until the heap no longer warms and then leave it to finish turning into compost. You may well see loads of red worms appear in the heap. These are friends helping and not anything to be concerned about.

Proprietary Composts
These are the composts you buy in bags in the garden centre or DIY store. Essentially made in the same way as you make compost at home but sieved to remove large particles, checked and balanced for acidity and nutrients and with added peat or peat substitute to improve the quality.

Without going into depth about the various mixtures, etc., available, you basically need just two types of proprietary compost: seed compost and multi-purpose compost. The first for seeds, of course, and the second for potting on or filling containers.

Since these are usually balanced for general gardeners, the addition of a small amount of lime (literally a dusting on a six-inch layer, well mixed before use) will usually improve the performance of multi-purpose compost.

It is always worthwhile paying a little more for quality. A good garden centre should be able to give you advice about brands. I personally favour Humax, which contains a product called Nutrimate that really does seem to improve growth rates.

Municipal Compost

If your local council has separate green waste collections it can be worth enquiring what happens to it. Usually it is sent to private contractors or a depot who compost it. You can often buy large quantities at very low cost which is a great way to improve your soil or fill deep beds with a good growing medium.

Fertilizers

NPK

Most fertilizers will contain three elements essential for growth: NPK which stands for Nitrogen (N) Phosphorus (P) and Potassium (K). These elements help plants grow in different ways and an understanding of this will help you when choosing the correct fertilizer for a plant or for a stage in the development of a plant.

Often when you buy a packaged commercial fertilizer you will see an analysis of the NPK content. An equally balanced fertilizer may be described as 5:5:5 – 5 per cent Nitrogen, 5 per cent Phosphorus and 5 per cent Potassium. You may also see Potassium described as Potash.

Nitrogen: the N in NPK

Nitrogen is used by the plant for the production of leafy growth and the formation of stems and branches. Plants most in need of nitrogen include grasses and leafy vegetables such as cabbage and spinach.

Plants in the bean family (legumes) have nodules on their roots where bacteria live that fix nitrogen from the air for use by the plant. They provide their own nitrogen fertilizer this way.

Shortage of Nitrogen in Plants – Symptoms
You can tell if your plants need nitrogen when their growth is stunted with weak stems and often they will have yellowed or discoloured leaves.

Application of Nitrogen
Nitrogenous fertilizers are quickly washed out of the soil by rain and need to be renewed annually.

Phosphorus: the P in NPK
Phosphorus is essential for seed germination and root development. It is needed particularly by young plants forming their root systems and by fruit and seed crops. Root vegetables such as carrots, swedes and turnips obviously need plentiful phosphorus to develop well.

Shortage of Phosphorus in Plants – Symptoms
Without ample phosphorus you will see stunted growth, probably a purple tinge to leaves and low fruit yields.

Application of Phosphorus
Phosphates remain in the soil for two or three years after application so the amount in a general fertilizer is probably enough. Add just before planting or top dress during growth periods.

Potassium: the K in NPK
Potassium (commonly called potash) has the chemical symbol K from its Latin name *kalium*. It promotes flower and fruit production and is vital for maintaining growth and helping

plants resist disease. It is used in the process of building starches and sugars, so is needed in vegetables and fruits. Carrots, parsnips, potatoes, tomatoes and apples all need plenty of potassium to crop well.

Shortage of Potassium in Plants – Symptoms

Plants that are short of potassium will have low resistance to disease, scorching of leaves and poor fruit yield. Tomatoes will really show the effects of a shortage of potassium.

Application of Potassium

Potash usually lasts for two or three years in the soil but for vegetable production (tomatoes, potatoes especially) additional will be required. This can be applied as a liquid feed (either a commercial one or one made from comfrey) for tomatoes or a specially prepared fertilizer, high in potassium for potatoes.

Micro-Nutrients and Trace Elements

Just as people require vitamins as well as protein and carbo-hydrates, plants require small amounts of various minerals to grow well. Usually these micro-nutrients will be supplied in the soil and organic fertilizers anyway and need not be a concern.

Magnesium deficiency is indicated by yellow patches between leaf veins and is most commonly seen in tomatoes as excessive potassium can cause a deficiency and we need to feed tomatoes heavily with potassium. The cure is to spray the plant with a solution of Epsom salts made by dissolving 30g in 0.5 litres of water.

Iron deficiency is indicated by yellowish foliage. If nitrogen does not improve the colour then try watering with 30 grams of sulphate of iron mixed in 5 litres of water.

Other trace elements like copper, boron, manganese and zinc are very rarely lacking. If you suspect any are, buy a balanced fertilizer containing them and apply as per the instructions.

Many organic growers find that seaweed extract such as SM3 sprayed onto plants will improve growth and disease resistance. The effect is similar to a vitamin pill, only useful if the basic nutrition has been supplied.

Types of Fertilizer

Chemical fertilizers can be bought in three main types:

- *Straight fertilizers* such as sulphate of ammonia or prilled urea (which just contains nitrogen), sulphate of potash (potassium) and super phosphate (for phosphorus). Usually you will not buy these individually, except sulphate of ammonia as a compost activator, or mix fertilizers since compound fertilizers are easily available.

- *Basic 'Growmore'.* This fertilizer was originally called National Growmore, developed to assist growers in the 'Dig for Victory' food production campaign of the Second World War. It simply contains NPK in equal parts 7-7-7. You can buy simple fertilizers balanced for different crops but just containing the three main constituents in different proportions such as 5-7-10.

- *Compound fertilizers.* These not only contain the basic elements but also a wide range of trace elements. They are often balanced to provide optimum feed for specific crops, such as Tomorite for tomatoes which is low in nitrogen and phosphorus but high in potassium and contains magnesium to compensate for the high potassium being likely to cause a deficiency in this.

You can also buy slow release fertilizers designed to dissolve gradually over the season from one application.

The benefit of chemical fertilizers is that they are available to the plant very quickly but the downside is that excess use tends to be washed into the environment and can cause problems in streams with excess algal growth. Excess use of nitrogen will cause plants to grow very lushly but become more susceptible to aphid attack.

Organic Versions of the Chemical Fertilizers
Fish, blood and bone is the organic version of Growmore. It releases more slowly, which helps to prevent over dosing, but this also means it is not effective as quickly as a chemical fertilizer so you need to think ahead and apply a fortnight before it is required.

Bone meal is low in nitrogen, very high in phosphorus but has no potassium. It encourages root growth and is especially recommended for use when planting fruit trees and bushes.

Dried blood is becoming harder to find but it is the organic version of sulphate of ammonia, being high in nitrogen but lacking any other nutrients.

You can also buy pelleted poultry manures which will be high in nitrogen and contain some trace elements as well.

A natural source of potash is wood ash. Although the exact chemical analysis will vary, generally you can think of wood ash as being a zero nitrogen, low phosphorus, high potash fertilizer: 0-1-3 NPK. So if you are burning wood, save the ashes and store in an airtight tin for later use.

Do remember that fertilizers are no substitute for a soil in good heart with plenty of humus but should be used to top up fertility.

Home-made Natural Fertilizers
Manure Tea
If you have a small quantity of animal dung (sheep being a favourite) you can use it to make your own liquid fertilizer. It will boost your crops but application is not as accurate as with bought-in proprietary fertilizers. However, the method is very simple: place the fresh manure into a porous bag (an old pillowcase will suffice or a hessian potato sack) and place in a barrel of water. Stir once or twice a day until the water is the

colour of strong tea (without milk!) and it is ready to use. The contents of the bag can be added to your compost heap and the tea applied to your plants.

This will be a high nitrogen fertilizer and is best used on leafy crops like brassicas although it will benefit almost anything.

Nettle Tea

Nettles are a difficult weed to deal with but the tea method, described above, will not only produce a worthwhile liquid fertilizer but also will ensure that the nettles are dead before adding them to the compost heap. Be warned though, this liquid can become quite smelly.

If you have a large patch of nettles growing nearby, it is worth taking a number of cuts throughout the year. Eventually you will weaken and even kill the nettles off which will enable you to bring the land into more productive use.

Comfrey

Comfrey, also known as Russian Comfrey, is a wonderful herb that will benefit your plot. I call my comfrey patch my 'compost mine'.

The best variety, in fact the only variety I would suggest you grow, is Bocking 14, so called because it was developed at the Bocking trial grounds of the Henry Doubleday Research Association (now known as Garden Organic). Henry Doubleday was an eighteenth century Quaker who first promoted the use of the herb and Lawrence D Hills, who founded the HDRA, was so impressed that he named the association after him and carried on with the research.

For an in-depth look at comfrey I would suggest reading his *Comfrey: Past, Present and Future* if you can find a copy as it is sadly now out of print. This fascinating book is full of information about the agricultural uses of comfrey as well as its horticultural uses.

The main reason I suggest Bocking 14 is that it is a sterile clone and so will not spread around the garden; for once established comfrey is very hard to get rid of. It is propagated from root cuttings, which can be purchased from Garden Organic. You need to be careful with comfrey – rotavate a patch of comfrey and in short order you will have dozens of plants for each one that was there before.

Comfrey will thrive in full sun or in partial to near full shade – there is usually a disused corner that will make a great site for your comfrey bed. It doesn't like thin, chalky soils and the roots go down a fair way, so dig deeply and break up the subsoil to get it off to a good start. Light sandy soils will benefit from organic matter. Being a fleshy plant it will need a lot of water and a soggy patch will be a plus.

Turn the soil over and remove any perennial weed roots. Comfrey grows very densely and will be difficult to weed. It does tend to shade out most weeds once established. If you have any manure – even poultry manure – fork this into the top six inches of the soil. Comfrey is great for soaking up nutrients and, unlike most plants, will not burn with raw manure.

You can obtain plants for most of the year but, if you can, plant in March, April, May or September for best results. I start the plants off in pots – just to get them off to a good start – and then plant out. You can plant directly but I like to ensure success, especially as they can cost over a pound each!

Block plant around 60cm–90cm (2–3 feet) apart and stand back. You will be surprised how quickly they grow. When the flowers appear, take a cut. Use a pair of shears and cut about 15cm (6 inches) from the ground. Comfrey has little hairs on the leaves, which can irritate. Not quite a cactus but near, so wear gloves.

Come winter the plants go dormant and a good layer of manure can be applied.

In the second year, your comfrey patch really starts to pay off. In the spring it will leap back from its winter sleep. Your first cut will help to get your potatoes off to a good start. After that you should get at least a further three cuts – even four.

To get further plants, push your spade through the middle of a plant and lever up a portion. Take root cuttings (about 5cm/2 inches long) and away you go again. Be careful as the bits left over will happily root wherever they fall.

USES OF COMFREY
There are three main uses of comfrey for the vegetable grower.
1. As a mulch it is especially good for potatoes and tomatoes. For potatoes, take a cut off the comfrey a couple of days before planting and leave to wilt. When you plant, lay the wilted comfrey in the bottom of the trench and cover with a thin layer of soil onto which the seed potatoes are placed before covering with more soil. As the potatoes grow, you can mulch the surface with cut comfrey; you can also do this around the base of outdoor tomatoes.
2. In the compost heap where it will act as an activator, just like manure, being so full of nutrients.
3. As a liquid feed it is superb, with the tea having a nutritional composition on a par with commercial tomato feed. Take some 6kg (14 lb) of wilted comfrey and place in porous sacks that are placed in 90 litres (20 gallons) of water in a barrel. Stir occasionally. In four to five weeks you will have a marvellous liquid tomato feed that you can also use on other crops. For tomatoes just water with it weekly after the fruit has commenced setting.

    The reason for the bag when making comfrey tea is that it stops the remains of the comfrey from blocking taps and spouts. Be warned: the smell is like an open sewer, but you will not notice this after your nose goes numb!

Lime
I am constantly surprised how many gardeners ignore liming. The acidity of the soil has a huge effect on fertility because the acidity of soil controls how available nutrients are to your

crops. The more acid the soil, the less the nutrients are available to your crops.

Most of our crops will do best in a soil where the pH is between 6 and 7. The letters pH stand for 'Power of Hydrogen'. The pH is a measure of the molar concentration of hydrogen ions in the solution and as such is a measure of acidity. For us non-chemist gardeners, the scale generally runs from 4.00, which is highly acid in soil terms, through 7.00 which is neutral, to 8.00 which is alkaline.

Lime also helps particles bind to each other and form larger particles in a process called flocculation; so adding lime will greatly improve clay soils.

Different soil types will behave differently so one vital tool for the serious gardener is a tester for acidity levels. You can also judge the acidity of the soil by the types of weeds that grow and their behaviour. Sorrel, creeping buttercup, nettle, dock and mare's tail are all signs that your soil is becoming or is too acid.

Soil testing kits and meters are easily and cheaply available in garden centres and DIY stores You can buy various types of test kit. Often you mix a soil sample with water then compare a colour change to a chart, but this is a bit of a pain for taking more than a couple of samples. I use an electronic meter, which is much easier, just requiring polishing and inserting into wet soil.

Whichever kit you use, it will come with instructions and will give you a reading. Never make a judgement on the basis of just one test. You may just have hit a spot with a particularly high or low pH. Take samples or test from a number of spots as that will give you a much better general view of your soil's acidity level.

Remember: To **LOWER** soil acidity we need to **RAISE** the pH value and vice versa.

To raise the pH and lower acidity or sweeten the soil, we add lime. To lower pH and increase acidity you can add sulphate of ammonia or urea which are high nitrogen fertilizers. From this you can see that adding manure will also lower pH and make the soil more acid.

It's counter to what you expect, but adding loads of manure year after year will actually reduce soil fertility by eventually making it too acid so the plants cannot access the nutrients. They become 'locked up' and lime will release them.

If you have ever had a pee (slightly acid) into a toilet with bleach (very alkaline) in it, you will have noticed there is an unpleasant reaction, Just the same if you mix your lime and fertilizer. They will at best cancel each other out in an unpleasant, to the soil, reaction. **So never lime at the same time you fertilize**.

Types of Garden Lime

Agricultural Lime or Garden Lime is made from pulverized limestone or chalk. As well as raising the pH, it will provide calcium for the crops and trace nutrients. Some recent experiments indicate that our soils may well benefit from the addition of rock dust, adding trace nutrients to the soil.

Dolomite lime is similar to garden lime but contains a higher percentage of magnesium.

Quicklime (Slaked Lime) is produced by burning rock limestone in kilns. It is highly caustic and cannot be applied directly to the soil. Quicklime reacts with water to produce slaked, or hydrated, lime, thus quicklime is spread around the land in heaps to absorb rain and form slaked lime, which is then spread on the soil. Such use is prohibited by the organic standards and, while fast acting, the effect is short-lived in comparison to garden lime.

How Much Lime to Use

How much lime to use will depend on your soil type and how far you have to raise your pH by. The chart opposite will give you a rough guide for how much ground limestone to use. For hydrated lime you only need between half and three-quarters the amount.

Do be careful: too much lime can raise your pH too far and an alkaline soil is as bad as an acid soil for yield. If in doubt, add some lime and recheck after a month.

When to Lime
It's usually best to lime your soil in the autumn and allow it to work its way into the soil over the winter. You do not want to lime when you have crops in the ground as the lime may well damage the crops. Build testing and liming into your rotation plan.

Amount of Lime to Raise Soil pH from 5.5 to 6.5

Soil Type	Kg/M^2	lb/yd^2
Clay	0.9	1.66
Sand	0.7	1.29
Light	0.8	1.47
Organic	1.1	2.03
Peat	1.7	3.13

8

WATERING

In these days of climate change it is difficult to predict what the weather will bring; one year the summer may have a drought, the next bring nothing but rain and flood. One thing is sure, however, in a drought there will be a hosepipe ban and watering the vegetable plot could result in a heavy fine.

Having covered how to cope with too much rain with drainage and raised beds, it is now time to look at how to cope with drought or even just a normal season. Many vegetables are spoilt for lack of water at the right time in their growing period which often coincides with low rainfall.

Drought conditions result in checked growth, tough and bitter leaves, stringy, cracked and misshaped root crops, as well as drastically reduced yield. To produce a good crop, no matter other factors, you must have an adequate supply of water available to your plants.

The first rule of coping with dry conditions is to have your soil in the best condition possible, with plenty of organic matter. This acts as a sponge, soaking up any rain and releasing it slowly to the plants. Sandy soils drain very freely, allowing precious water to disappear, so the humus will really be of most benefit there. Clay soils with low humus however have a nasty habit of drying to a hard pan on the surface, so any rain just runs over the surface without penetrating below where it is needed.

With clay soils particularly, you can help in a drought by hoeing the surface. Not only does this prevent weeds competing with the crops for the available moisture but breaking up the surface prevents water being drawn to the surface by capillary action where it evaporates away to no benefit.

Mulching exposed soils between rows will help keep moisture in the soil. You can use leafmould, straw, grass cuttings, etc. Do ensure selective weedkillers have not been used on the mulching materials though.

Shade can help reduce water needs in a scorching summer. Plants, like us, sweat when it is hot to control temperature. This is known as transpiration in plants and can be significant. Some crops like tomatoes and lettuce do not enjoy blazing hot temperatures and if you can erect some makeshift shade it will improve things.

Having done what you can to minimize water loss, we can consider when and how to water. If the plants are wilting, then obviously it is urgent but don't be fooled into thinking that you must water just because the soil looks dry. Especially if you have hoed, the surface may conceal quite damp soil below the surface. Just stick your finger in and see if it comes out dry or use a trowel to scrape a small hole. If the soil is dry below 5cm or 10cm (2 or 4 inches) it needs watering.

Do not follow the practice of watering little and often. The evaporation loss will be a high proportion of the amount used, reducing effectiveness and little will penetrate to where it is needed below the surface. The crops' roots will follow water so you encourage shallow rooting.

It is much more effective to split the plot into sections, watering heavily in one area each day. You should not need to water properly more than once every three days or longer, depending on the crop and your soil. Some crops, like tomatoes, are exceptionally sensitive to irregular watering and lack of water followed by heavy watering causes skin cracking and blossom end rot. Other crops, such as potatoes, require a lot of water.

You should look to provide the equivalent of 10–15mm of rain in a watering at a minimum. That is 10–15 litres per square metre and many crops will need double that. This is an awful lot if delivered by watering can so concentrate the water directly on the plants. Half burying a 2-litre plastic bottle with the base cut off, neck-end down, by the stem enables you to deliver the water quickly and accurately to where it is needed for those tomatoes, courgettes, etc.

Better still, especially in a drought, is to use leaky or seep hoses. These are just like a normal hosepipe except they allow water to seep slowly out. They are best used by drawing a shallow trench, about 10cm (4 inches) deep, laying the hose in and covering with soil. You can buy various connectors and link the hoses, enabling you to water a section at a time. Generally you should space them about one metre (40 inches) apart or you can lay one per raised bed.

Because they are under the surface, evaporation losses are minimal and the water spreads from side to side down to the roots. How long to leave the water running is something you learn to judge as the time will be influenced by the water pressure and the hose.

Sprinklers are easy to use and will deliver water over a wide area with just the effort of connecting them up and moving down the plot as you go. It is hard to estimate how much water has been delivered this way so take a straight sided container (an old tin will do the job) and mark out with a felt tip a line 1.5cm and 3cm above the base on the inside. Just stand the tin level in the area covered by the sprinkler and you can accurately measure the delivered amount.

There are lots of different sprinklers on the market.

Fixed sprinklers, often with a dial to change the spray pattern, can be purchased very cheaply but they are light-weight and tend to be moved by the pressure of water being sprayed out.

Rotating sprinklers are more effective but if the base is at an angle the spray will be uneven and again they may tip over.

Oscillating sprinklers are effective and tend to have a firm spray pattern and be stable in use.

Best of all is a good quality pulsating sprinkler. Often supplied with a spiked telescoping tripod to raise the head above the foliage, by means of various screws you control throw distance and the spray pattern can be adjusted. They tend to be quite expensive but last for years.

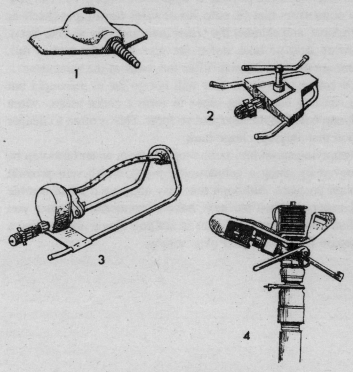

Fig. 22. Various types of sprinkler.
(1) Fixed.
(2) Rotating.
(3) Oscillating.
(4) Pulsating.

There is little point discussing how to water if we have none
to deliver. The water companies seem happy to allow millions
of gallons to go to waste through leaks but at the first sign of
decent weather along comes a hosepipe ban.

However you may feel about the ban, it is not worth risking
the fine for breaking the law so you need to secure your own
supply. Every year, even drought years, water falls from the
sky so we need to catch it and hang onto it.

Installing guttering onto sheds and greenhouses and piping
into water butts can provide a significant supply. You can also
buy connectors that fit onto housewater downpipes, such as
Rain Sava, and channel the water automatically to your butts,
allowing it to go back down the pipe when the butt is full.
There are models that will filter the water at the same time.

Of course, one water butt will not go far in a drought but
you can buy connecting pipes to form a chain where, when
full, one butt fills the next and so forth. This is often a cheaper
option than buying a large tank.

Supplying sprinklers and hosepipes from water butts can be
achieved by using a submersible pump which will provide
enough pressure. Although this may all seem a lot of trouble
and expense, when we next have a wonderful summer you
will still have crops and there is nothing illegal about using a
hosepipe filled from your own supply.

9

GREENHOUSES AND POLYTUNNELS

Fig. 23. Greenhouse.

Greenhouses

Greenhouses and polytunnels are immensely useful to the vegetable grower and well worth the investment they entail. Although they both provide a protected growing environment they have different characteristics and uses.

The greenhouse is more of a workshop where we start seedlings off and grow plants on that will move outside, usually equipped with staging and, if possible, supplied with electrical power and heating. On a cold wet day, working in the warm dry greenhouse is a definite bonus for the gardener. The polytunnel is usually larger and is more of a giant cloche, providing a sheltered environment to grow plants in directly to maturity. First we will look at the greenhouse.

Where to Put the Greenhouse
One of the things people often forget is to give a little thought to where they are going to position their greenhouse. The correct situation of the greenhouse will make a huge difference to its utility for you.

A normal greenhouse will not usually require planning permission but a lean-to greenhouse on the house may be counted as part of an extension or there may be rules on siting a distance from the boundary. If in doubt, call your local council who will tell you exactly where you stand.

On an allotment, it will depend on your individual site's rules. Just check with your site rep or manager, who will be able to give you guidance.

Both on the allotment and in some gardens, you need to consider security. Some kids just love the sound of breaking glass, and throwing stones over the fence is an easy sport. So consider the position and, if there is a real threat and you cannot site out of harm's way, plastic glass may be the best answer for you.

Allow room to get around your greenhouse. Trying to fit a new pane of glass in a confined space is not easy and, if your greenhouse is by a path, try to set it back to allow plenty of room to get past with a wheelbarrow.

You need as much light as possible so site the greenhouse away from buildings and trees or bushes. Apart from shading your greenhouse, leaves will get into the gutters and sticky honeydew dropping from insects in a tree above your house will foul the glass, causing dirt and grime to stick creating more problems.

Avoid north-facing slopes because the light will never be as good as you want.

Whilst you want to be some distance from trees, hedges, fences, etc., these can also be useful if they are between the greenhouse and the prevailing winds. Reducing wind will really help keep the temperature up in the key times of spring and autumn.

Avoid building at the base of a slope as these are often frost pockets where cold air collects in a layer. This will cause your greenhouse to be colder, defeating the object of having one. The greenhouse needs to be level so level ground is best.

Ensure the land is well drained because this will enable you to cultivate the border soil at any time of year without it being too sticky.

The ideal greenhouse will have water and electricity laid on, even gas if you want central heating, which I have seen in some greenhouses. So do take the availability of services and how you will run them to your greenhouse into account.

Some say you should orientate your greenhouse north to south and some say east to west but for the average home greenhouse it doesn't really matter, so don't worry about it. The exception is, of course, a lean-to greenhouse where the ideal is to have the house facing south on a north wall but even a north-facing greenhouse is better than no greenhouse!

What Sort of Greenhouse?

Having decided where to put the greenhouse, the next question is what type of greenhouse? Most modern greenhouses are constructed of aluminium framing with glass to the ground and this style is probably the best all round. Aluminium will last for many years without any sort of maintenance; it doesn't rot, warp or rust and is robust if assembled correctly initially.

Wooden greenhouses can be very attractive features in any garden but the wood does require maintenance to keep it from eventually rotting. These are available with glass to ground as with aluminium houses or with a dwarf boarded wall on the sides. This does prevent making use of soil borders though.

The choice will come down to your situation and budget. For practicality and cost, aluminium is favoured but for aesthetic appeal wood cannot be beaten.

Normally the house will be glazed with horticultural glass. You can buy houses glazed with safety glass if you have concerns about this. Ask for specific information from the manufacturer.

Another option is glazing with twin-walled polycarbonate sheeting instead of glass. The benefit is that the inbuilt insulation effect will keep the house warmer in cold spells but reduced light transmission can make seedlings drawn and seems to slow the ripening of tomatoes.

There is no ideal size for a greenhouse. At times you will always wish you had a larger one when the border is crowded out and the benches full. So the best advice is to go for the largest you can.

Building the Greenhouse

Whatever type of greenhouse you decide upon, you will need a firm base for it. Especially with aluminium greenhouses it is important that it be square and level, for if the base is distorted, the greenhouse will be distorted and this will cause glass to crack and fall out. Damaged panes of glass should be replaced immediately because, once the wind gets in, the house can be reduced to twisted frames and broken glass. A square house will resist the winter storms, the wind flowing over. Never leave the door open in windy weather because of this.

Most greenhouses seem short of headroom and building up the sidewalls will generate that headroom. One layer of breeze block or a dwarf wall of two or three bricks will be sufficient. The easiest method is to use wooden beams, 20cm by 10cm (8 inches by 4 inches), to form the base. These can be laid directly onto solid ground or on a foundation trench filled with concrete. Double check that the distance between diagonal corners is equal to know it is square and use a decent spirit level to ensure it is level.

Inside the house you can have a solid concrete floor, paving slabs laid as for a patio or a soil floor with paving slabs laid up the middle. For a greenhouse where much will be grown in the borders you can use wooden beams to turn them into deep beds.

I favour one border for direct growing and the rest of the house paved to support staging, etc.

New greenhouses will be delivered from the manufacturer with full instructions for erection which should be carefully followed. Aluminium greenhouses are quite easy to build, so long as the base is firm, and erection will take less than a day on average.

Second-hand greenhouses can often be picked up for very little, even free on occasion. Ideally, you want to dismantle the greenhouse yourself. This means you can check the condition and that all parts are there. Buying a dismantled greenhouse you really don't know until the end if everything is there.

Start by removing the glass. Most of the sheets will be a standard 61cm square but mark unusual sized sheets with a felt tip pen and note down where they go. Next mark major components and note where they are. A rough sketch will help you recall when you re-assemble, and a few photographs can be very helpful.

You will probably need to buy packs of nuts and bolts and glazing clips. They magically vanish between one site and the next. You may also need to replace the glazing seals. These can be purchased in rolls that you cut to size quite cheaply. Ebay is often a good source.

Always, and I cannot stress this enough, always wear gloves handling glass. Glass weakens with age and hairline cracks can cause a pane to break when you least expect. Work slow and safe.

Ventilation

The worst problem with greenhouses is that they get overly hot and humid. Often they do not come supplied with enough vents and you should fit an additional vent at low level. A louvre window that replaces a pane of glass is a good option. Opening and closing the windows by hand to regulate the temperature is possible but it is far easier to buy automatic vent openers that react to the temperature and do the job for you automatically.

Temperature Control

In the summer even the open vents will not keep the temperature to reasonable levels and plants can be scorched by hot sunlight. You can whitewash the house with special shading such as Coolglass but this will need to be wiped off again at the end of summer. Purpose-made net shadings can be fixed internally or externally to reduce the sunlight and you can even buy external bamboo blinds that unroll over the roof.

In the early spring, your concern will be to keep the temperature up in the house, at least frost-free.

There are various insulators that you can buy or you can use bubble plastic packaging material for much the same effect but less cost. With a large house you can make a curtain to just keep half the house warm. Without insulation, even keeping the greenhouse frost-free in cold weather can be very difficult and expensive.

The most cost-effective heater for a greenhouse is paraffin-fuelled. The fuel is still relatively cheap, the heaters inexpensive and they are ideal for allotments or situations where electricity is not available. The drawback with them is that they produce condensation and do smell. You should not spend time in the greenhouse with the heater running as the fumes are unpleasant and they may produce carbon monoxide which is dangerous.

Electric heaters cost more to run, although with thermostatic controls not as much more as you may fear. It is important to get a heater suitable for use in the greenhouse environment where water is around.

Finally, you can use gas heaters, either portable propane or even mains gas-powered systems. They're wonderful if you can afford the installation.

Heated Propagators

With an electricity supply you can utilize a heated propagator in your greenhouse, effectively a mini-greenhouse in the greenhouse. The temperature in the propagator may be 20° Celsius, when in the house it is just 3°C or 4°C and outside below zero.

Heated benches where special cables are laid under sand, along with thermostatic control units and special grow lighting above, enable you to turn winter into summer. This is beyond the needs of the normal vegetable grower but is the sort of system used by specialist show growers looking for a gold medal.

Staging and Shelving

A wide range of benches can be bought as well as shelves designed to fix into the channels in aluminium-framed houses. A nice task for the dark days of December is to read through manufacturers' catalogues, admiring if not buying the ingenious accessories available.

Constructing your own benching just using wood is a satisfying and perfectly adequate low-cost option. Benching raises the plants above the colder floor area (heat rises), as well as being convenient to work on for potting up, etc.

Water

Much is made of using soft rainwater in a greenhouse although this can be a problem in that rainwater often contains disease spores causing far more problem than clean mains water.

The temperature of the water is another matter. Mains water

will usually be around 5° Celsius whatever the air temperature – perhaps a little cooler in winter and warmer in summer but around that temperature. So watering your plants directly with mains water will drastically reduce the temperature of the soil, the reverse of bottom heat and check their growth.

The ideal is to store clean water in the greenhouse for long enough for it to warm up to the ambient temperature. Twenty-four hours is usually enough. The water can be stored in cheap plastic watering cans or a water butt. You can buy slimline water butts that will fit in the corner on a stand, using the butt to fill your cans and topping up as required.

A benefit of a water butt in the greenhouse is that it will hold warmth from the day, releasing it at night to moderate the temperature in the house.

A range of watering systems is available. One includes a simple 10 litre bag and tubes where you hang the bag, which is filled with water that trickles through the tubes being slowed by restrictors so entering the compost slowly over a couple of hours.

Capillary systems where water is drawn into a mat, laid in a waterproof tray, to be taken up by the plants in their pots and modules are very useful, especially if you are away for a weekend. They ensure seedlings never dry out but neither is the compost soaked.

More sophisticated irrigation and misting systems are available but they are overkill for the average gardener.

The amount to water depends on the following factors: the temperature, the amount of sunlight and the amount of foliage the plant has. It really is a matter of judgement and use of the 'moisture measuring meter mark one' – your finger. You really cannot beat inserting a finger into the soil to see how damp it is.

Occasionally you will have a hot day when you're away and the compost will dry out. In an ideal world this doesn't happen but we're all human. Once dried out, peat and peat-substitute-based composts are difficult to get wet again. Water just runs through and leaves the compost mainly dry. With smaller pots and trays, you can soak these for an hour or so up to the brim in a bucket and the compost will wet again but with larger pots this is difficult. The answer here is a drop, literally just a drop, of washing up liquid in the water. This is technically known as a wetting agent and reduces the surface tension of the water, allowing it to penetrate the soil better. Rather than just pouring water into the pot, use a fine rose on the watering can to spread the water over the surface, helping to start re-opening the pores in the soil allowing the water in. With a bordered greenhouse where plants such as tomatoes are growing directly, rather than pouring water onto the surface, insert a plastic 2-litre bottle with the base cut off neck-down a few centimetres into the soil by the plant stem. Water and feed directly into the bottle, which will ensure the water goes to the roots, leaving the surface dry.

This reduces evaporation loss and so prevents the atmosphere becoming damp in the greenhouse. Past practice was to positively ensure a damp atmosphere in the greenhouse but this practice encourages fungal disease to develop.

Another benefit of keeping the border surface dry is that it discourages the germination of weeds.

Polytunnels

The polytunnel is increasing in popularity as more people discover the benefits. Unlike a glass greenhouse, the polytunnel provides a diffuse light and is usually cooler in summer and warmer in winter than the glasshouse. The drop at night may well be lower as well. It is used rather like a giant cloche to extend the growing season of a wide variety of plants and protect them from extremes of weather.

Some crops, like runner beans, rarely do well in a polytunnel due to the lack of pollinating insects but nearly anything that can be grown outdoors can be grown more reliably over a longer season in a polytunnel.

Polytunnels are available in sizes ranging from that of a

small greenhouse, 2 metres x 2.4 metres (6½ feet x 8 feet), to professional models 8 metres (26 feet) wide and up to 27 metres (90 feet) long. They are cheaper, size for size, than a greenhouse and the advice is to buy as large as you can fit in and afford. A 4.2 metre (14 feet) x 6 metre (20 feet) polytunnel would be superb for any home grower.

They really consist of two parts, the frame (which is a permanent, long-lived component) and the cover (which will last on average anything from four to ten years). Replacement covers cost around 15 per cent to 20 per cent of the cost of a complete house. Various types and strengths of cover are available: standard clear polythene covers, UV stabilized to resist degradation in sunlight, through to covers designed with thermal properties to improve heat retention and with additives to control the condensation of water on the film.

It is worth carefully checking the technical specification for the frame; support hoops should not be spaced more than 2 metres (6½ feet) apart, a little less is better. The steel tubes that form the hoops should be no less than 35mm in diameter and the steel should be high tensile. The apex height is important but more important is the height at the sides. High-sided tunnels, where the sides go straight up for a metre before beginning to curve, will provide far more usable growing space internally.

Properly erected they are stable and will resist high winds, often better than a greenhouse but note the qualification 'properly erected'. Building the average polytunnel is a two-person task over a couple of days and the manufacturer's instructions must be followed to the letter. With larger tunnels, extra help to put the cover on will be needed, so hold a barn raising.

When positioning the polytunnel, the same criteria as for the greenhouse applies but pay more attention to the soil condition and possible flooding. Crops are grown directly in the soil in a polytunnel. Do remember that you cannot secure a polytunnel; a vandal equipped with a penknife can enter easily and silently, causing very expensive damage in moments.

Ventilation is usually through the doors where fine netting is used rather than polythene allowing air ingress. You can heat a polytunnel but normally they are unheated.

Various accessories are available including support bars and base boards. Base boards make tensioning the cover an easier task than burying the film in a trench, which is the normal method. Support bars are needed for exposed sites where the tunnel will be subject to high winds and special bars enable things to be hung like hanging baskets.

Irrigation and misting systems are available but rarely justifiable for the home grower considering the expense. As with the greenhouse, raising water temperature is beneficial although not to the same extent. Leaky hose-based systems, especially when combined with a time control system, enable the grower to take a week or two away in summer knowing that the tunnel will be fine.

Because you are growing directly into the soil in your tunnel and demanding a lot from it, it is important it is prepared properly. Double dig initially and add lots of organic matter. Because you cannot increase the soil level much in your tunnel, removing some soil and replacing with compost each year will enable you to maintain the highest quality and this reduces the risk of the soil becoming sick since maintaining a rotation is difficult if not impossible in a polytunnel.

Be careful of over fertilizing though; there is no rain leaching the nutrients from the soil and, especially with chemical fertilizers, salts can build up, negating your efforts.

Growing techniques are similar as for containers and raised beds. Maximize the use of the space by starting crops off in modules and pots, transplanting into soil when ready. As soon as one crop comes out, another can take its place. Successional sowings scheduled so that a new planting is available as the old is removed is most effective.

Think three dimensionally: taller crops towards the centre

of the tunnel, root crops to the edge but don't be afraid to interplant short and tall plants to utilize your space further. You really need to get a good return on your investment.

As with a greenhouse, try to avoid surface watering where possible, to prevent a humid atmosphere encouraging botrytis. Leaky hoses buried a few centimetres under the surface and sunken bottles are the way around this.

Polytunnels are one of those things in life that you don't think you need but when you have one you wonder how you ever managed without it.

10

PESTS, PROBLEMS
AND PROTECTION

Slugs and Snails

By far the worst pest to every vegetable grower is the slug. It doesn't matter where you grow or what you grow, the slug is waiting to devour your crop before you do. They're not fussy eaters but they do prefer tender young seedlings. Often a grower will claim a row failed to come up when the truth is that the slugs have eaten the seedlings.

Slug Pellets

Slug pellets have had a bad press, the theory being that the poisoned slugs will be eaten by birds, frogs and other helpful creatures who feed upon slugs, and poison them in turn. The other concern is that the pellets may be eaten directly by pets or even children and poison them.

If used correctly there is no risk of poisoning pets or children unless they are really determined. The pellets should be scattered thinly over an area, not dumped in piles; this means to harm a pet it would need to eat one and then find the next, etc. Piling them up is counter productive anyway as they contain an attractant and so the slug will find each pellet. The pellets contain a repellent to discourage animals from eating them and the blue colour apparently repels birds as well.

There is no evidence of birds, etc., being actually harmed by secondary poisoning but it is a theoretical risk. The active ingredient is Metaldehyde.

Because of the effectiveness and convenience of slug pellets a version containing a different active ingredient, ferrous phosphate, has been developed that addresses these concerns and is certified for use in organic systems. In some ways I think these pellets are superior and seem to last longer in rainy weather which counteracts them being more expensive.

Used correctly you will not need more than one pack per season – scatter thinly!

Nematodes

This is a biological control where you purchase microscopic worms (*phasmarhabditis hermaphrodita*) that are a slug parasite. The drawbacks are that you need to use them at the correct time when the soil is warm enough, they do not work as well on heavy clay soils and they are expensive. The benefit is that they are very effective, wiping out the slug population both above and below ground. Even using slug pellets, crops like potatoes can be spoilt by small slugs working underground but the nematodes will kill the lot. Unfortunately, the slugs return after six weeks or so and another application is required. You can buy programme packs where the nematodes (trade name Nemaslug) are posted to you at the optimum application time for three treatments.

Traps and Hunting

Organic growers often extol the virtues of using jars sunk into the ground or purpose-made slug traps filled with beer to trap the slugs which, one presumes, die a happy death drowning in the beer. They do work, certainly attracting slugs which become a smelly sludge quite quickly.

You can also trap slugs under half grapefruit or orange skins, even pieces of wood on the ground for the slug likes to hide away from predatory birds in the day, coming out at dusk to feed.

Going out into the garden at dusk with a torch you can hunt the slugs and snails, picking them up to dispose of later. If you keep chickens, they will appreciate the protein.

Personally I think life is too short and the combination of safe pellets and nematodes is the ideal control.

Copper Barriers

Slugs apparently will not crawl over copper and you can buy rings of tin copper to place around plants and tape to stick to pots to prevent slugs climbing into them. This assumes, of course, that no slug eggs are hatching in the compost in the pot in the first place.

If you find copper attractive and money is not a concern, then by all means give copper barriers a go.

Pigeons and Other Birds

Fig. 24. Wood pigeon.

Although some other birds may cause some damage to your crops, by far the worst culprit is the wood pigeon. They do tremendous damage to brassicas, especially in winter and spring when food is scarce. They can literally reduce a cabbage to a few stalks in a morning before you get out of bed. It's not just brassicas; they enjoy peas and beans, even turnips and swedes, as well as fruit and berries in season. Seedlings are a particular delicacy in their diet.

Having seen a pair of pigeons sitting on a scarecrow, it obviously has little deterrent effect. I've also seen them alight on CDs hung on strings to deter birds, so that's another great theory that didn't quite work in practice. Pigeons are both persistent and clever birds. They soon become habituated to scarers and ignore them. Shouting will scare them away until you turn your back, when they'll be back in short order.

The only answer is to net your crops. You need to ensure the netting is supported (so that they cannot press it down onto the crop to gain access) and that it goes down to the ground (or they will find their way under). Remember they can destroy a crop in a day, so net before it is too late, especially in winter.

A frame, with wire attached that can be fixed into the ground forming supportive sides over which a net can be spread, makes a convenient movable cage. Permanent plantings of fruit are best protected with a walk-in cage. These can be purchased in kit form or constructed with a little DIY knowledge.

Not all birds are a problem. For example, the robin, who appears as we dig over the ground, helps us by feasting on the exposed pests in the soil. So please don't engage in trapping or suchlike. It is not only counter productive but also illegal.

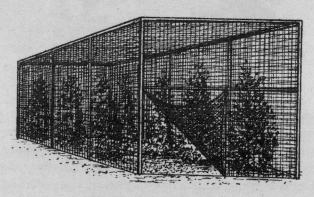

Fig. 25   A vegetable cage.

Rabbits

Strangely enough the one crop that seems immune to the rabbit is the lettuce. Otherwise they can be a terrible problem, especially in numbers. Since rabbits can burrow, the answer is to erect wire net fencing which is buried at least 20cm (8 inches) into the ground and 60cm (2 feet) above ground.

Rats and Mice

These can be a problem, although generally not a major one; the mouse notably for eating newly sown peas. Both can spread a serious disease, Weil's disease, which can be fatal, so they are not creatures we want to encourage into the garden.

They can be attracted by cooked food, especially meat, in the compost bin and so those should never be added. Controlling rats and mice usually involves traps, with differing degrees of success, and poisons. You should be exceptionally careful with poisons since they can also kill pets and even children. If in doubt, contact your local council who will at least provide specific advice and can often deal with the problem for you.

Moles

Moles rarely cause too much of a problem in the vegetable plot but there are various deterrents and traps available on the market.

Cats

Cats of themselves are actually beneficial on the vegetable plot. The cat wandering about or even snoozing in the sun will deter the pigeon from landing to eat your crops. The cat will also solve any mouse problem for you, although many cats find discretion the better part of valour with regard to rats. The tom cat's habit of scent marking his territory also deters rats who prefer not to find out how good and brave a hunter he is.

However, the cat's preference for newly dug soil as a toilet is the cause of much annoyance to the gardener. His presents are not what you want to find in the soil. You can deter cats by using pepper dust on the soil. Also clear 2-litre bottles filled with water have been known to scare them off. Their distorted reflection is taken to be a strange cat approaching and so they retreat.

A water pistol, even one improvised from a washing up liquid bottle, is effective. The cat isn't hurt by it but as they loathe water they will depart and probably not return.

Carrot Root Fly

The carrot fly not only affects carrots but parsnips and even celery as well. The fly's maggots cause the damage, killing seedlings and burrowing just under the skin of more mature plants, leaving brown tunnels behind. Parsnips left in the ground through to January can be ruined as the maggots continue to feed, causing more damage.

The flies produce two generations in a year and are active in April/May and July/August, which almost ensures they can get at our crops. You can try sowing outside of those times (in February, March, June, September and October) but it's not an absolute guarantee by any means.

The fly is attracted by the smell of carrots and is most active in the day so thinning, which bruises foliage and releases the scent, is best carried out late in the day to avoid their notice. Inter-planting with stronger smelling onions is supposed to confuse the fly but evidence is mixed on this.

Because the fly tends (notice that, it tends) to fly near the ground, putting up a vertical barrier is often advocated to keep the fly off. The carrot bed is surrounded by some sort of solid fence at least 70cm (28 inches) high but not more than 1 metre (40 inches) wide. This is fairly effective, but not 100 per cent. Growing your carrots high in containers like half barrels above the 70cm (28 inch) level can also help by keeping your crop out of reach.

The best barrier is to grow under fleece, especially in the prime danger months. The fleece can cause problems itself, however, crushing the foliage and encouraging mildew to develop so support it above the plants with hoops or plant canes with an empty bottle on them. You will need to remove the fleece to cultivate and this is best done late in the day to avoid our pest.

There are no chemicals available to the amateur gardener to control the pest but resistant varieties such as Flyaway have come onto the market. If carrot fly is a particular problem in your area, resistant varieties may be your best bet, combined with barrier methods.

Club-root

Club-root is a serious disease that affects brassicas. It is caused by a soil-borne organism and once in the soil it can remain for twenty years so conventional rotations have little effect. It is easily spread, just walking from an infected patch onto a clean patch of land will infect the soil. It can also travel on plants, so do not accept brassica seedlings where the source is not known to be clean.

The first sign is a wilting of plants, especially in dry weather. The plants fail to develop well and often fail to develop a crop. Examining the roots you will notice swellings and roots that look knobbly, like advanced arthritis which is where the old colloquial name of 'fingers and toes' comes from.

Although no chemical controls are available to the gardener nowadays, the good news is that some resistant varieties are coming onto the market and more are being developed.

Once you have club-root on your plot I'm afraid you are stuck with it. The good news is that you can continue to grow brassicas successfully with careful cultivation.

First practise good hygiene. When your brassicas are finished, carefully remove all the roots and do not compost them, either treat as household waste or incinerate. Remember that the affected family includes radishes and mustard, so do not use a mustard green manure and promptly remove radishes that have grown too large and woody to use and do not compost them. This will reduce the reservoir of the organism in the soil.

Start your brassicas off in modules using bought in composts to which a small amount of lime has been added and pot up to 7.5cm (3 inches) and then in at least 12.5cm (5 inch) pots before planting out. This allows the plant to develop a good root system prior to infection.

Club-root thrives best in acid wet soils so ensure your brassica bed is well dug, adding grit if need be to keep the soil free draining. Take the pH up to 7, neutral, or even as high as 8.5 by adding lime (see page 86). Before planting, dig a hole at least 30cm (1 foot) deep and in diameter and then dust with lime to whiten the soil in the hole. Fill this with bought-in multi-purpose compost and then plant in this.

This method has been proven to work and enable good quality crops to be taken – even prize-winning cauliflowers. It is a lot of work and you may feel that just growing completely in containers is your best solution. Do try those resistant varieties, but remember this is resistance not immunity.

Cabbage Root Fly

The damage is caused by the cabbage fly maggot rather than the fly itself and, once again, chemical control is unavailable to the home grower. The damage to the roots weakens the plant and the symptoms above ground are similar to club-root but the characteristic root swelling of club-root will not be present.

The fly needs to lay its eggs by the plant stem so keeping them away from that is effective. Usually this is done by making a collar from old carpet or carpet underlay. Cut a 15cm (6 inch) circle of carpet and cut a straight line to the centre. When you plant out, place this around the stem and check it remains in position through the season.

Butterflies

Beautiful as the butterfly may be, its caterpillar will happily eat the leaves off a cabbage for you. They are fairly easy to control without resorting to chemicals or biological controls. Regularly check under the leaves for clusters of eggs. These will be seen as small (approximately 2mm) yellow or white spheres. Just wash them off or crush them with your finger.

If you miss a batch, then you can pick off the caterpillars by hand and dispose of them away from the plant. It is no more work than spraying the caterpillars with a chemical (Derris) or a nematode-based biological control.

Aphids

The aphid family of some 500 species, including greenfly and blackfly, causes damage to a wide range of plants from cabbages and broad beans to aubergines and tomatoes in the greenhouse.

They feed on the plant by inserting their syringe-like mouth into the plant and sucking the sap. This weakens the plants and can pass viral disease from plant to plant. They produce honeydew; a sticky waste which forms a growth medium for moulds and is prized by ants who actually farm the aphids, protecting them from predators in return for a food source.

Outside, the answer is to wash them off with a water spray or, more effectively, with insecticidal soft soap. Derris is an effective chemical control for aphids.

Aphids generally go for the lush, growing tip of the plant and over-use of nitrogen fertilizer will produce just the growth they love. With broad beans, which always seem to be hit with blackfly, once they have grown just clip off the growing tip and dispose of it with pests attached.

The natural enemy of the aphid is the ladybird and you can buy ladybird larvae as a biological control for use in the greenhouse.

Whitefly

Whitefly are quite common on brassicas but they do not actually cause much damage to the plants. Disturbing the plants can cause a cloud of the small flies to appear. Treat as aphids if you think they are harming your crop.

In the greenhouse they can be more of a pest and here you can hang yellow sticky cards between the plants. The whitefly is attracted to yellow for some reason and once it lands on the card it sticks and dies.

An effective, more effective than chemical, control exists for greenhouse use in the shape of a parasitic wasp, *Encarsia formosa*. This tiny wasp does not sting people, so have no fear. It does, however, lay its eggs into the whitefly scales and will reduce the problem in short order.

Spidermite

The red spidermite is so tiny, just half a millimetre across, that the leaf damage is usually the first thing noticed. Leaves become bronzed, wither and die. Check they are the cause with a magnifying glass: you're looking for tiny red or yellow spiders. A specific biological control, *Phytoseiulus persimilis*, is available, and washing with insecticidal soap is moderately effective. Usually they are not too damaging but heavy infestations require action to avoid significant crop damage.

Flea Beetle

These small beetles, about 3mm in length, jump like a flea – hence the name. They eat holes in the leaves and usually cause more damage to small plants and seedlings than larger mature plants. They seem to love radishes and will attack other members of the brassica family.

They are susceptible to a spray or dusting of Derris. One good method of control is to coat a piece of cardboard with treacle and wave it just above the leaves of a row of radishes. The beetles get stuck to the card which can then be disposed of or provided as a treat for chickens.

Mildew

Mildew, seen as a white powdery coating on the leaves, weakens and may kill the plant. It is common in dull humid weather and in greenhouses with reduced ventilation. Different forms attack different plants but outside of the greenhouse it is rarely a serious problem for the vegetable gardener.

Various chemical controls are available but you need to check they are licensed for use on the particular crop you are growing.

Potassium bicarbonate, mixed at 5–10g per litre and applied as a spray weekly, is generally effective.

Blight

Blight is famous for being one of the causes of the devastating potato famine in Ireland in the 1840s. It really can devastate a potato crop and also kills tomatoes.

It is a fungal disease, *Phytophthora infestans*, and spread by airborne spores, developing when the weather conditions are correct. Spread is very rapid throughout the crop when temperatures are above 10°C and humidity is over 75 per cent for two days or more, known as a Smith period. Rain then washes spores from the leaves down into the soil where they can infect the tubers.

The effect is that the foliage develops brown patches on the leaves and sometimes in a few days all the foliage is dead. Infected tubers rot and the smell is both revolting and distinctive.

Usually early potatoes are not affected, as the weather conditions are rarely correct, but the maincrop potatoes are often hit by blight. Tomatoes in a greenhouse may well escape infection when outdoor tomatoes have been infected, as the lack of wet foliage in the greenhouse does not allow the blight to gain a hold.

Blight can be prevented by spraying every 10 to 14 days with either the traditional Bordeaux mixture or a modern fungicide such as Dithane. Once the blight has a hold, no cure as such is possible although applying the fungicide may slow progress a little. Accordingly the sprays should be made before a Smith period occurs and blight is likely.

Although Bordeaux mixture is a traditional blight preventative, being made of just copper sulphate and lime and it is approved in organic systems (at time of writing), I would strongly suggest that Dithane is actually safer and better for the environment and for you than a mixture containing copper.

Once blight is seen in the foliage, the best course of action is to remove it immediately and burn or otherwise dispose of it (do not compost). This, hopefully, will prevent the tubers being infected. Leave the tubers for two or three weeks and then harvest.

Once harvested, it is important to check for blight in the tubers as it will spread in store. In bad cases, wash the seemingly unaffected potatoes and re-check after a couple of weeks.

Potatoes vary in their blight resistance and recently new varieties have come onto the market that are almost immune. These are based on the Hungarian Sarpo line and include Sarpo Axona and Sarpo Mira. More varieties based on the line are undergoing tests and should be on the market soon.

11

THE VEGETABLE YEAR

January

Fig. 26. January.

January usually brings hard frosts but, with a bit of luck, you will have the opportunity to catch up with those winter jobs you are behind on. It may well be your last chance before really cold weather sets in and the ground is frozen solid, so don't procrastinate. If the day is fine, get out into it. If nothing else, you will feel better for the fresh air.

Check your stored vegetables carefully, for rot will pass easily one to another. The saying, 'one bad apple spoils the barrel', has a lot of truth in it. Empty the sacks of potatoes, checking them for rot and for any slugs that might have been overwintering unnoticed. Your nose is a good indicator; often you will smell rot, even if it is not immediately apparent to the eye. A squeeze will confirm a potato has gone rotten.

Strung onions should also be checked; rot usually starts from the underside of the onion and this is the place to look at closely.

If you are storing your vegetables in a shed or outbuilding, make sure the temperature does not drop too far. A maximum and minimum thermometer will tell you what the low was in the night. You do not want your vegetables to go below 2° Celsius and certainly do not want them to freeze. Freezing and thawing will cause cell breakdown and rot will start. Potatoes will acquire a sweetish unpleasant taste as well.

If you have electric power to your storage area, you can buy thermostatically controlled electric heaters that will maintain a low temperature or you can even just use a 100 watt or 150 watt light bulb with the bulb holder at low level overnight, shielded with a tin to shade the light. It is not the light but the heat we are using the bulb for and often it will be just enough to hold the temperature above freezing.

Although January is definitely not a month for outdoor sowing and planting, you can try starting some summer cauliflowers in a frost-free greenhouse or even a coldframe.

Unless you have specialist equipment, it's always a gamble sowing in deep winter, for who knows how cold it may get? Sometimes the gamble pays off and sometimes you have wasted a few seeds and a bit of compost.

Although the specialist growers (those chaps and I'm glad to say a few ladies nowadays), who grow fantastic perfect vegetables for the major horticultural shows, are in full swing, we are still waiting for the season to start. Don't forget that they have climate-controlled greenhouses, equipped with special lighting to increase the day length to the optimum for each crop.

If you really want to extend your season, you can build a wooden-sided coldframe insulated with polystyrene tiles or sheets (which are often available from electrical retailers as discarded packaging). This will be surprisingly warm even in cold weather.

The white colour of the polystyrene reflects light onto the plant, which is helpful. Don't forget to cover at night with some form of insulation, although even this small chore can be dispensed with by using some bubble plastic under the lights or even old double glazing.

When mankind moved to an agricultural economy it became important to know whereabouts in the year you were. Seeds need to be planted at the right time. Sow too early and bad weather will destroy the crop, too late and it will not have sufficient time to mature for harvest.

So, to find where he was in the calendar, ancient man realized the variable length of the day could give him that help. The two most important dates were the shortest day and the longest day. The shortest told him where he was in winter and the longest day in summer. Two other dates could also be worked out from the day length, the equinoxes where day and night are approximately equal length.

In the UK these dates are:

Winter Solstice (Shortest Day): 21 December
Vernal or Spring Equinox: 20 or 21 March
Summer Solstice (Longest Day): 21 June
Autumnal Equinox: 22 or 23 September

Of course, the plant kingdom had worked this out first. Many plants use the length of the day to judge when to flower or set seed. Different varieties of plants will react to day length in different ways. That is why our onions in Britain are geared towards a 14 hour period whereas varieties more suitable for the tropics use 10 hours of day length as a trigger for maturity.

Basic to a plant's growth is daylight. Like a solar power system, the plant uses the energy from sunlight to power its growth. Temperature, nutrient levels in the soil and water are all important but without sunlight plants will not grow. The more sunlight, the more energy is available for the plant to power that growth. Growing too far outside of a plant's natural season will often fail, since the plant knows there is not enough daylight.

In January there is only around eight hours of daylight, so, even if the temperature is warm enough, there is not enough solar power available for growth for many plants.

The rough guide to day length below, which varies according to where you are, shows why our growing season really takes off in March and tails away in September.

Daylength in Hours	
January	7.5–8.5
February	9–10.5
March	11–12.5
April	13–15
May	15.5–16.5
June	16.5–17
July	17–16
August	15.5–14
September	13.5–12
October	11.5–9.5
November	9–8
December	7.5–8

One task you can start in January is building a traditional runner bean trench. Since runner beans like a rich damp soil, this old method is still effective, especially where you have sandy soils. Dig a trench where the beans are to go; around

20–30cm (8–12 inches) deep and wide is ideal. Line with newspaper and then add kitchen waste, old brassica stalks (assuming you have no club-root on the plot), etc., into the trench until it is nearly full, covering with soil to keep off any rats. You don't need to do it in one go; a section at a time is best if only to stop the papers blowing away.

When you come to spring, the compost materials will have sunk and this provides a depression to help with watering the beans later in the year.

Start chitting your potatoes in January (see page 213) to ensure good strong sprouts to get them off to a good start when you plant out. If it is looking like a mild year, you can try planting two or three tubers of a first early in a greenhouse, either in a border or bags. Alternatively, you can use a coldframe. I am fortunate to have a plastic, raised bed base, about 1m x 50cm and 20cm high (40 inches x 20 inches and 8 inches high), to which a twinwall polycarbonate coldframe attaches that provides shelter and depth for a really early crop, so long as the weather isn't too drastic.

You have to accept some risk of failure when you stretch the season, but it's a low-cost gamble.

What you could be eating now
Apart from your crops in store, you could still be pulling leeks. Parsnips and swedes store well in the ground, so long as it isn't so frozen to make harvest impossible. Your winter brassicas will still be there, although there are limits to their hardiness in extreme weather. A later sowing of Brussels sprouts can still be producing well into January and beyond.

Beet leaves (perpetual spinach), possibly true winter spinach and chards should still be around, as well as curly kale. Some of the kales are exceptionally hardy – just scrape off the snow and harvest!

Celery should be available and possibly celeriac; Jerusalem artichokes, if not dug up and stored, will be in the ground,

along with salsify and scorzonera. Possibly non-forcing and
certainly forcing chicory can be adding its distinctive flavour
to a winter salad along with hardy lettuce.

February

Fig. 27.   February.

February is often the coldest winter month although spring
is just around the corner. More than any other month, what
to do in February will depend on weather. It's a month where
you can be frozen solid under snow at the start but almost
pleasant by the end. The nights are drawing out and longer
days mean we can start planting but only if the weather
allows.

Do not slavishly follow instructions to sow or plant outside
in February; think of the conditions. Cold and wet ground will
not germinate seeds, just kill them off. You can, however, get
around this to some extent by using cloches for a week or so
beforehand to warm and dry the soil.

Another soil-warming method is to cover your soil with
black plastic sheets that will absorb what sunlight there is and
keep the water off. I mention this as I have seen it done but do
you really want a plot covered in sheets of plastic?

If you're up to date with the winter tasks, and February is
your absolute last chance to catch up, then the one job left is
to clean the greenhouse and coldframes ready for March when
the season should move into full swing. Replace any broken

panes, double check that the clips are in place, etc., and then give it a good wash down with Jeyes Fluid. A window cleaner's squeegee is good for the job. Cleaning the glass improves the light transmission so vital in the spring when light levels may be low and the Jeyes will kill off any pests hiding in the nooks and crannies.

Since you are washing the greenhouse, you may as well take the opportunity to wash out your pots. These are going to be used next and good hygiene helps prevent disease spreading to the seedlings. By wash, I mean just dunk and shake before stacking them to dry.

Double check the pH of the brassica patch and, if need be, add lime to raise it up to 6.5 or even 7.0. This will give the lime a chance to settle in before you start planting. This year's potato bed will benefit from a little extra well rotted manure as well. You can rotavate or fork it in next month.

If the weather is good, you can do some early sowing outdoors, although it's best done under cloche unless it is particularly mild.

Broad beans and early peas to be ready for harvest in May and June can go in, as can Jerusalem artichokes. Shallots should, if possible, go out early but they really do benefit from protection, fleece or cloche until they have got going, as will turnips.

If the weather is severe, you can still start the broad beans in 8cm (3 inch) pots filled with multi-purpose compost under glass. Even in fine weather this method shows better results with higher germination rates, so the row can be planted in March.

Summer cabbage and cauliflowers should be started under glass, the coldframe being sufficient. One seed tray with an insert to provide 15 modules is more than enough for this first sowing. You are only looking to get four or six plants off to a good start. Hardy lettuce can be started under glass as well, to provide an early salad crop along with rocket and some radishes.

The greenhouse border can be brought into productive use, as long as you have it cleaned. A row or two of early carrots (the Nantes variety is ideal) will produce usable roots from the first thinnings in 5 weeks and can come out in 8–10 weeks, by which time the beds will be needed for the tomatoes and so on.

Conventional advice is to sow parsnips now, but you will get much better germination rates in March or even as late as April when the soil is in better condition. They will still be ready by the time the next frosts arrive.

Onions from seed can be started towards the end of the month, probably more reliably indoors on a cool window sill, but be careful not to shock them when they are moved out into the greenhouse or coldframe. If you didn't plant your garlic cloves out in November, then pop them in now. They like a cold spell so the frosts will not harm them.

Your potatoes should be chitting well; check them over. It is surprisingly easy to have them upside down and you want the sprouts at the top towards the light. One tip is to spray them at fortnightly intervals with a seaweed solution such as SM3. The theory is it helps produce stronger plants, although I haven't noticed any real difference.

What you could be eating now
Fresh from the ground you could still have leeks, parsnips, swedes, salsify and scorzonera, assuming you can get your root crops out of the ground. The cabbage family should be providing some sustenance with winter cabbage, early purple sprouting, kale and Brussels sprouts being available. Beet leaves (perpetual spinach) and chards will be available, all being well.

Other crops you may have: celeriac and celery, chicories, Jerusalem artichokes, hardy lettuce and spinach.

March

Fig. 28.   March.

March is the month where things really heat up for the gardener and the garden – the true start of the growing season. In fact, the start of the year used to be The Feast of the Annunciation, 25 March until 1752 in Britain when we adopted the Gregorian calendar and started our year on 1 January.

Caesar may have had the ides of March to contend with but we have that uncertain weather to trouble us. The day's length is such that the plants want to get going but the ground must be right for success. March is said to arrive roaring like a lion and leave like a lamb, so patience is a virtue this month as we wait for the spring lamb.

Don't panic if the weather is bad, as the plants will catch up.

Although it may not be ideal for our pampered vegetables, the weeds will certainly be springing up. If conditions permit, get the hoe moving and keep it moving to kill them young.

Your cloches can be moved on from those February planted crops when they are established but you're likely to be short of crop cover so use horticultural fleece, laid a week or more before sowing or planting, if the temperatures are low, to warm the soil.

Even if you sowed broad beans and peas in February, there

is nothing to stop you successionally sowing another batch to be ready later than the first.

March and April are usually the right time to establish an asparagus bed if you are starting from crowns. Although it is a crop that takes two years before it starts producing, it will be there for many years so don't skimp on preparation. If you are waiting on your order, you can take the opportunity to prepare the bed anyway.

If not planted last month, the Jerusalem artichokes can go in now.

In good years, the middle to the end of March is when the first early potatoes can go in but April is a safer option. If you have a comfrey patch, with luck the first cut can go into the trench under the potatoes with a little soil on top. Take the cut a day or two before planting to allow it to wilt. In short order the comfrey will be providing nutrition on a par with purpose-made potato fertilizer to get them off to a good start. If it is a slow season and the comfrey isn't ready, you can lay the first cut in-between the rows as a mulch after planting.

The earthing up process (see page 214) will provide some protection for the potatoes from late frosts but you can still lose foliage so covering with fleece is recommended.

Directly sow the following, under cloche if the weather is bad. Don't forget that setting up the cloche a few days to a week beforehand will warm the soil and, if it is wet, allow it to dry and be more workable.

- Beetroot (small fast varieties for eating in June rather than larger storing varieties).
- Peas, including the mangetout and petits pois varieties.
- Parsnips.
- Carrots.
- Radish.
- Spinach beet (beet leaf).
- Early turnips.
- Cut and come again lettuce and salad leaves.

- Spring onions.
- Onion sets.
- Shallots.

In modules start off:

- Lettuce.
- Sprouts (early varieties to be ready for September).
- Summer cabbages.
- Celery.
- Early cauliflowers.
- Onions from seed (keep around 10–12° Celsius; do not let them go above 15° Celsius)

In a heated propagator if you have one, or inside the house on a window sill, you can start off your tomatoes, peppers, aubergines and greenhouse cucumbers. This needn't take much room since you can start them in 7.5cm (3 inch) pots, shallow if you have them, and move them on to individual pots or modules when they are big enough to handle. Electric propagators can be bought quite cheaply, and unheated propagators designed to fit in a window sill are a satisfactory solution. As celeriac needs a long season it is best started at the beginning of the month.

What you could be eating now
Any leeks you have left in the ground should come up now. They can be frozen for use in soups and stews if you have too many to use up.

Parsnips too should come out of the ground in early March before they try and re-grow. You can store them for a few weeks in damp sand but they know the season and will not hold for long. Prepare some parsnip chips and freeze them if you want to enjoy this winter vegetable out of season.

You may have spinach beet and chards available, the last of the late Brussels sprouts, winter cauliflowers, kale, swedes, salsify and scorzonera but all these are coming to the end now. Spring cabbage may well be ready to cut late in the month.

Keep checking your purple sprouting though, that should be in full flush. In the greenhouse you can have some lettuce and, with luck, the thinnings from your early carrots might provide a delicate treat worthy of a top restaurant.

April

Fig. 29. April.

April is great: the soil is warming up and spring should definitely be here. Do keep an eye on the weather forecast though; even in the south of England a cold snap and snow are not unknown in April and the occasional frost is to be expected. Keeping horticultural fleece on standby in case of cold weather is a good idea. Although some years April seems more like June, the first rule is never trust the weather.

Do remember that the weeds are springing into action, so keep the hoe going. Don't forget that a sharp hoe is the best friend a gardener can have. Just slide it back and forth slightly below the surface of the soil and you'll stop the weed seedlings in their tracks.

On those days when April showers turn to monsoon, re-check your stored crops.

There's quite a list to sow and plant outside, especially if

March has not been suitable and, even if it has been reasonable, the successional sowings continue.

Easter usually falls in April and Easter is the traditional planting date for potatoes, which is more to do with holiday time for the workers rather than anything else. As Easter is a movable feast, you can see it little matters exactly when you plant them as long as it is around this time.

It's not too late to get Jerusalem artichokes planted, although you are pushing the edge now so the sooner they go in the better. It's also the time to start that totally unrelated, except by name, globe artichoke.

The last sowing of broad beans can go in the ground directly or into pots for planting out later. Another sowing of peas can go in and, if you want to impress, you can start a few dwarf runner beans in pots to grow in the greenhouse. Unlike our normal runner bean, these dwarf plants will thrive in a large, say 20cm (8 inch), pot and provide an early treat.

The normal runner bean is not at all hardy and so we need to plan carefully. Plants outside that have grown too large to be protected will be killed if a late frost arrives, so start off in pots towards the end of the month. These can then be planted out mid-May and, if a frost should strike, will still be small enough to be protected with fleece or even newspapers.

Dwarf French beans can be started now, again in pots preferably in the greenhouse but definitely under glass. Just start a few because the risk of losing them is high this early in the season and the May sowing often does best, arriving as the frost risk is completely past.

Climbing French beans can be started in pots. Treat just as runner beans and remember that frost risk. The Borlotti bean, which is grown for the dried bean rather than the pod, needs the longest season you can provide so, if you can only protect a few climbing beans, these are the ones to start first.

Onion sets and shallots can go out as well, but do be quick with the shallots since they do like a long time in the ground.

Any onions from seed, started in modules, really should be ready to go out by now as well.

Continue successional sowings of the brassicas in modules, moving on to small pots (8cm/3 inch) and then to 15cm (6 inch) pots if you are cursed with club-root before planting out. Your brassicas:

- Broccoli.
- Brussels sprouts.
- Cabbage (winter and summer varieties).
- Cauliflower.
- Kale.

Don't forget to keep sowing lettuce and salad leaves every fortnight or three weeks to keep a continuous supply, along with radishes and spring onions. A successional sowing of kohlrabi, beetroot, turnips, spinach beets and chards can go in along with true spinach.

Carrots do well sown now but the carrot root fly is around. Covering with fleece is the best protection against this pest but do ensure the edges are to the ground so it doesn't sneak in.

Late in the month you can sow salsify and scorzonera. Although they are low producing and difficult to prepare for the cook, they really do have a special flavour.

Your comfrey patch should be doing well now, providing a cut for the potato trench or a mulch if the comfrey is lagging behind your planting plan. Comfrey provides a potash-rich fertilizer with deep roots taking up nutrients from the subsoil but it will benefit from some fertilizer itself. To maintain its growth some nitrogen-rich manure, even raw chicken manure, will help it no end. If you have no manure, then a sprinkling of sulphate of ammonia around the plants will have the same effect.

If you've not already done so, get those greenhouse tomatoes, peppers and aubergines started early in the month.

Better late than never. You also start the outdoor cucumber off in April, bringing it on to plant out when all danger of frost has passed by.

Towards the middle or end of the month, start the sweet-corn in pots or toilet roll inner tubes closely packed in seed trays. Chitting the seed always produces good results and saves the effort of potting dead seed. This assumes you will have cloches available at planting out in mid-May to insure against the risk of one late frost and to get them away well.

Don't forget that as the weather warms not only do the weeds start to grow but our enemy the slug is becoming active. Protect against them in the way you choose but make sure you do something or you will wonder what happened to those seedlings you planted out yesterday that have vanished overnight.

What you could be eating now

We're in the 'Hungry Gap' between the last of the winter crops and the start of the early crops but there are still a few things available: late sprouting broccoli, cabbage, cauliflower and chards for example, plus you may have some early salad crops and carrots from the greenhouse border.

If the weather has been kind and you planted some fast early potatoes in January under cover, then you could be enjoying the first small new potatoes.

Hopefully your stored roots and home-frozen supplies mean you will not be putting money into the supermarket's tills.

May

Fig. 30. May.

May is one of the busiest months in the kitchen garden. The soil is warm and everything should be growing well. Unfortunately, the weeds are growing well too so there is no time to relax. Do watch out for a late frost; many growers have been caught out and lost their recently planted beans, etc. Keep that fleece handy just in case.

If you do not have any horticultural fleece, you can use old net curtains, bubble wrap and the traditional newspaper as a method of insulation when a cold night is forecast.

From your garden diary you will get to know when your frost risk has passed – mine is 27 May so by June I no longer worry.

There are two main cultivation jobs you need to keep on top of in May. The first is to keep on top of the weeds. There is nothing as dispiriting as looking down a plot covered with weeds. Try splitting your plot into sections and tackle a section a day for a week. If you do two sections in one day you may have Sunday off!

The other important cultivation job outdoors is to thin out directly sown carrots, parsnips and other root crops. Although you can close space to a degree in containers and raised beds, with normal growing it is important to observe the recommended spacing. These have been calculated to maximize yield, so when you sow a row of carrots and lots come up you need to remove the excess.

You can get an extra crop of carrots by leaving them at half the final spacing and then thinning alternate plants a few weeks later to provide fingerlings. Thinning carrots will bruise foliage and you will notice that carrot smell. So will the carrot fly whose scent detection system guides her radar-like to your crop. Thinning late in the day will help (as they are settling down for the night), as will getting the fleece back on as quickly as possible, of course.

There is a lot to sow this month, with some new crops and the successional sowings to be continued so that you enjoy fresh vegetables at the peak of perfection. If it is a dry May, it is a good idea to soak your seed drill before sowing and then just water with a fine rose after covering with soil.

French beans sown in rows under cloche will do well in May. If you cannot cloche them, then sow towards the end of the month to ensure the seedlings will not be caught by a late frost. Runner beans and climbing French beans can be sown directly as well: drop two seeds per supporting cane to ensure at least one plant per cane eventually.

Successional sowings of the brassicas carries on, continually moving on to pot and planting out:

- Broccoli.
- Calabrese.
- Cabbage.
- Cauliflower.
- Kale.

The maincrop peas are sown towards the end of the month and the beginning of June. These usually climb highest and will need the sturdiest of support. It's worthwhile setting the stakes and netting before sowing because, when the plants start growing, you may damage them in the erection process.

If you did not get salsify and scorzonera sown in late April, pop these in early this month. Plant out the celeriac and celery when ready.

Continue with successional sowings of beetroot, carrots, kohlrabi, turnips, swedes, salad leaves, lettuce, radish and spring onions.

You can sow sweetcorn directly if the soil is warm enough although it will need some protection. If you do not have cloches available, then you can use clear plastic lemonade bottles with the base cut off sunk into the ground over the seed, neck-end up, to provide a mini-cloche. Planting out sweetcorn started indoors can also take place, but ensure they are protected against frost.

The courgettes, squash, marrows and pumpkins should be started off in May. Sowing in pots in the warm is more successful than direct planting and, since you will only want a couple of each plant, is the way to go.

They take off quickly so be prepared to pot on if you cannot get them out when ready. Courgettes are very productive and two or three plants will be quite enough to ensure the end of the season is met with a sigh of relief from the family. You can have too much of a good thing.

Invariably at this time of year the 'Three Sisters Method' is raised in the gardening press. The method was developed by Hopi Indians in the south-west USA who needed to maximize food production in a desert. Sweetcorn was sown in a hole, with a climbing bean beside it and some squash planted between the rows. The bean, being a legume, provided extra nitrogen when the lump of excrement, which was dropped first into the hole, ran out of food for the corn. The corn provided support for the bean and both provided shade from the blazing sun for the squash, reducing water use.

I have no doubt this method works well in those conditions but having tried it three times in variable British summers, my strong advice is to forget it. The corn does well but the beans are hard to get at and the squash certainly suffers from the shade, resulting in reduced crops at best.

Planting out of brassicas as they come ready continues this month and leeks can be planted out in their final home when they are about pencil thickness although usually these are not ready until June.

The greenhouse tomatoes, peppers, cucumber and aubergine can go into their final home now – either border, growbags or large pots. It's too early for outdoor tomatoes unless you can keep them under cloche.

What you could be eating now

Depending where you are and what you planted, you should have some salad crops ready and carrot thinnings, along with early turnips. If you tried very early potatoes undercover, you may well be getting meals from these if luck was with you. Winter cauliflowers, spring cabbage, sprouting broccoli and kale should all be ready now.

One real luxury crop you may have, if you're in your third year of growing it, is asparagus. Fresh English asparagus may taste sinful, but it is good for you and low-calorie as well – except for the melted butter, of course.

June

Fig. 31. June.

Flaming June should bring us a hot sunshine-filled month, with the risk of frost having passed, and those in more northerly parts should be able to catch up with those in the south. We're also moving towards the longest day – June 21 being the summer solstice – so there is plenty of daylight to let you get on with things. There is a lot to do in June but the rewards for our efforts are coming in the harvest.

As with May, we really need to keep on top of the weeds so keep that hoe moving. Check your directly sown crops – carrots, parsnips, beetroot, turnips, etc. – and thin as necessary. You should be safe from the carrot fly now but she will be back next month and it is probably easiest to leave your defences in place, especially if she has not heard that she's not supposed to be about in June.

This can be a dry month so keep an eye on the need to water. If the soil appears dry, then check under the surface, either by scraping some soil away with a trowel or pushing your finger in. If it comes up dry, you need to water. Don't forget to water when required. A person can live for three weeks without food but only three days without water. Plants are little different except that one day with no water available can be enough to finish some plants.

You should be planting out brassicas now: broccoli and calabrese, Brussels sprouts and summer cabbage.

If you have started beans in pots, both runner and French, these should go into the outside too. Leeks should be ready to move to their final position this month. Ideally, they want to be about pencil thickness. Don't follow the old guidance to trim the leaves and roots when transplanting leeks. It has been proven to be of no benefit and is counter-productive. Celery can go out now as well, if you didn't get it out in late May.

Outdoor tomatoes can go to their final position in mid to late June as well. When moving plants from greenhouse to outdoors, it is a good idea to condition them to the move. Take them out in the day and put them back at night for a few days or move from greenhouse to coldframe and then to the plot. This avoids shocking the plant by a sudden and drastic change in climate.

In the greenhouse, keep pinching off the side shoots from

your tomatoes and keep an eye out for pests such as aphids, whitefly and red spider mite. If you are subject to attack by these pests, it is worth checking out biological controls as these are perfectly safe to use and, used correctly, more effective than traditional chemical controls.

Many of the chemical controls of the past are no longer available anyway so the organic alternatives are now the mainstream choice.

On the subject of pests, the infantry brigades of slugs and snails are attacking at ground level so take action to keep them down and don't ignore the air force of birds that are dropping from the skies to eat your crops. Don't forget the netting.

The butterflies are about now as well. Beautiful as they are, check the undersides of your brassica leaves for the yellow or white eggs that will hatch into caterpillars and devastate the plant. You can squash them, wipe or wash them off easily at this stage.

June is the last month for sowing many crops as we pass the longest day and head downhill again. Planting out from successional sowings in modules and pots is maximising the use of your space but you are probably wondering where to fit things in by now. Don't be too precious about rotational plans; plans are great until they bump head on into reality. If something gets planted in the wrong place, it will probably be OK. Do be ruthless, if you have lettuce starting to bolt – off to the compost heap with them and plant something else in the space. Incidentally, if you have a glut of lettuce, you could try cooking lettuce with peas or even make hot lettuce soup.

French beans can be directly sown now and, if frost has caught you by surprise, killing your first sowing of runner beans, it is not too late for a second try.

The maincrop peas, climbing the netting for 1.5 metres (5 feet), go in now, as do the maincrop carrots if they're not in already.

The beetroot sown at the end of June can be left to swell and store with the root vegetables, whilst the earlier sown are taken at golf-ball size to go in salads. The swedes go in at this time as do the turnips but remember that swedes are brassicas and can be vulnerable to club-root. Add extra lime in the soil and start off in fresh multi-purpose compost. Varieties such as Marian show resistance to club-root.

Your squash, pumpkins, courgettes and marrows should go out this month. Take the opportunity to prepare for planting at the start of the month.

If your sweetcorn are not sown yet, then you need to get going with them. The longer the season, the better with sweetcorn. Even if the weather is fine, leave them under cloche until the leaves are pushing the edge as the extra heat will help.

If they look a little yellow and sickly, try sprinkling 25ml of sulphate of ammonia or 50ml of dried blood around each plant and watering it in with a fine rose. It's surprising how the nitrogen boost can help bring the plant on, even if it has been checked with cold weather.

The outdoor cucumber can be started directly or in a pot to go out late this month. The flavour of the outdoor varieties seems more pronounced than the greenhouse types.

What you could be eating now

There will be plenty of salad crops available: lettuce, spring onion, radish, etc., summer cabbage and early carrots. With carrots, the later thinnings can provide a great addition to a salad or just be steamed with a cooked meal. Beetroot, young turnips and summer spinach may all be welcome fresh additions to your diet and, with a little luck, the early peas could well be cropping in June, especially in the south. November-sown broad beans may well be on your plate – the immature beans are a good way to introduce the bean to those who claim to hate them.

Best of all will be the first early potatoes and asparagus. The humble spud ceases to be a filler on the plate when you grow your own and it is fresh. It is transformed into a treat.

Just take up a plant at a time and move down the row as you
need them. This gives them time to develop further. You may
need two plants for a family meal to start with but that's OK
because you will get double the yield by the end of the month.

Resist the urge to crop the asparagus heavily in the early
years. It will give you more as time passes but only if you let
it establish properly.

July

Fig. 32.   July.

July is usually one of the driest months so a lot of time may
be spent watering. You can reduce water loss and so save
yourself some time. Mulching with a layer of organic matter
will help preserve moisture but may encourage slugs so you
will need to take action against them.

Another good method of preventing water loss is to hoe.
This not only kills the weeds but breaks up the top of the soil,
stopping water from being drawn to the surface by capillary
action and evaporating.

Although the hectic sowing of the first part of the year is
past, there are still things to sow, plant out and happily
harvest. Those early potatoes should be coming out of the
ground now and, although they do not store as long as the
maincrop varieties, they will store until you have finished
eating them.

When you harvest your potatoes, take care to remove all the tubers. Any left will not only sprout next year and become a weed but will also be a reservoir for disease and potato blight spores. It's often worth forking over a few days after harvesting potatoes because more seem to appear miraculously.

It's a good idea to follow the potato crop with a green manure crop. Agricultural mustard, broadcast by hand, is best so long as you don't have the dreaded club-root on your plot because it is a member of the brassica tribe and will help to keep the club-root going in the soil.

The mustard will help to reduce eelworm by preventing them from breeding in season. Wireworms are unaffected by mustard but they are most common in new plots where grass was growing although they can be a pest on any plot. They eat into the potato, leaving tunnels behind, and severe infestations can ruin the whole crop.

If the weather is dull and moist, then there is a likelihood of potato blight striking. Apart from growing resistant varieties like the new Sarpo, there are only two courses of action to take. First, trust to luck and hope it misses you which is not quite as silly as it sounds. In an average year, it is very much a case of luck deciding. The second course of action is to use preventative sprays like the traditional Bordeaux mixture which is still approved for organic use despite the fact that copper is a poison and the non-organic Dithane is, in my opinion, better for the environment and the people eating the crop.

Keep an eye on the potatoes and, if you spot characteristic brown blotched leaves, remove that foliage immediately and incinerate. There is no cure for blight available to us and, once started, a spray may delay the inevitable but that is the best we can hope for.

Blight will also strike tomatoes, which seem to suffer more than potatoes. If moving from plot to greenhouse, try to avoid spreading the disease by not handling blighted foliage and then going into the greenhouse. More often than not, the greenhouse crops will miss the blight.

Crops to sow in July
- Beetroot.
- Spring cabbage.
- Chicory.
- Chinese cabbage.
- Carrots.
- Kohlrabi.
- Lettuce.
- Peas (use an early variety to have them ready before the season ends).
- French beans.
- Radishes (winter varieties as well as salad types).
- Spring onions.

If they've not gone out in June, there is still time to get leeks planted out. If you find you've more small leek plantlets than you want to grow on, you can eat them. They work well in stir fries instead of spring onions.

Continue successional plantings of brassicas – calabrese, cabbage, cauliflowers and kale. When planting into a space that a previous crop has occupied, do remember that the soil has already used up nutrients and apply a general fertilizer beforehand to counteract this.

For greenhouse crops and outdoor tomatoes where we demand a huge crop from the plants, it is critical to keep feeding each week with a liquid fertilizer. Comfrey feed is as good as commercial tomato feed and free to produce.

It's a good idea to give your maincrop potatoes a feed as well. A major cause of poor crops with maincrop potatoes is that they run out of food. They are a very greedy plant and a boost now will pay a dividend in tubers. Tomato food is ideal for them, being part of the same family, and watering between the rows with 10 litres per 3 metres of comfrey feed will do the job. If you don't have comfrey feed and don't want to spend out on liquid tomato food, then 50–100g of general fertilizer, like fish, blood and bone or Growmore, will provide the boost they need.

In the greenhouse, watch the temperature and ensure good ventilation. It can get incredibly hot in a greenhouse with strong sun and can scorch your plants. You should also consider shading the house, either with blinds, films or with a shading wash.

If you're manually opening vents, remember that the sun is up at dawn; if you sleep a little later than that, then invest in automatic vent openers.

If you find yourself with some time, turn the compost heap. Just empty out the bin and refill it to ensure everything is thoroughly mixed, watering if dry. This will introduce air, and speed up the decomposition process.

What you could be eating now
All your hard work is really giving you a reward now; the harvest is in full swing, providing you with the following:

- Broad beans.
- French beans.
- Runner beans.
- Cabbage.
- Carrots.
- Cauliflower.
- Celery.
- Courgettes.
- Cucumbers.
- Kale.
- Kohlrabi.
- Lettuce.
- Onions.
- Spring onions.
- Peas.

- Early potatoes (second early salad potatoes may be ready as well).
- Radish.
- Spinach.
- Tomatoes.
- Turnips.

August

Fig. 33. August.

August, with a little luck, brings us the best of the summer weather but, being the traditional holiday month, it can be hard to keep on top of the vegetable plot with a fortnight away, even if a neighbour can be persuaded to water as required.

The second early potatoes will all be coming up now, along with early maincrop potatoes and, hopefully, you have escaped the blight. It is important to watch out for Smith periods (see page 117), spraying as a preventative if you wish. If you do get an attack of potato blight, the best method to preserve the crop is to remove the haulm and dispose of it, then leave the potatoes in the ground for a fortnight to stop the spores getting onto the tubers. It's best to harvest potatoes fairly early in the day, rinse them off as they come from the ground and then leave in the sunlight for a day to dry off thoroughly and harden the skins before storing.

Sort carefully and place perfect specimens into hessian or paper sacks in a cool, dark but frost-free place. Damaged tubers should be used first, before they have a chance to rot and spread their rot to the rest of the sack.

It's worthwhile emptying the sacks after a few weeks or a month and check that there are no potatoes going off. Discard these before they rot the sack. You might like to pop a few slug pellets into the sacks as well. It's amazing how the slugs can appear, no matter how careful you are. If you are concerned about slug pellets, remember that these ones are in store and present absolutely no risk to wildlife.

Once you've harvested your potatoes, rather than leave the soil bare to grow weeds through to winter, add green manure. Even if it only stops the weeds from growing, it's worthwhile.

As spaces develop that you are not going to fill this year, try sowing some dwarf French beans as a green manure. The seeds are cheap enough and even if you have enough beans to feed an army, the plant produces a fair amount of leaf and stem, plus the roots, as with all legumes, have nodules containing bacteria that fix nitrogen from the atmosphere. Free fertilizer as well as organic matter can't be bad. Unlike most green manures, French beans can be used in even small patches.

There are still quite a few things you should be sowing in August, such as spring cabbage and Chinese cabbage, which is a late crop, as well as hardy lettuce. Although we think of lettuce as a summer crop, it is a surprisingly hardy plant and under cloche and in the greenhouse can easily be available for a Boxing Day salad rather than some tasteless import from sunnier climes.

Sow spring onions like White Lisbon winter hardy which will grow, albeit slowly, to add zing to that salad, along with some fast-growing radishes.

Late spinach can be sown in August along with a last sowing of kohlrabi and turnips.

Plant out the savoy cabbages and cauliflowers to grow on for the earliest crop, as well as hardy kales.

Your runner beans will be at the top of the canes now, so pinch out their growing tip to encourage bushier growth below. Pick all runner, climbing and dwarf beans regularly except for the haricot varieties, such as Borlotti, where we want the bean rather than pod for table.

Stop tomato plants now to encourage fruit to swell and ripen. Stopping is the process of cutting off the growing tip so the plant's energy is not diverted into foliage from fruit. Keep your tomato side-shoots in check; you want tomatoes not masses of foliage. Ensure they are watered regularly. Drying out prevents the plant from taking up sufficient calcium and the deficit causes blossom end rot.

Keep on top of the pests. Aphids and blackfly are a particular problem in the greenhouse, although they are certainly about in the open plot as well. You can control them with pesticides or just wash them off many plants with a strong jet of water. A squirt with soft soap solution will do no harm to the plants and will reduce the numbers by stopping the pests breathing. In the greenhouse, biological controls are most effective and don't forget the traditional sticky yellow cards which attract the whitefly.

Keep an eye on your brassicas for butterfly eggs and caterpillars. Most of these will be under the leaves towards the stem in clusters of little yellow/white balls. Pick or wash them off before they develop and dine on your dinner.

Turn your compost. The warmth will be helping your compost break down and turning it out to in will ensure even breakdown. Water if it is dry as the microbes need some water but don't make it absolutely sodden. The plastic tubular bins can benefit just from a stir around with a fork if you are pushed for time.

What you could be eating fresh now
The harvest should be doing well, providing you with both fresh vegetables and vegetables to store through the winter.

- Aubergine.
- Beet leaf (chards and perpetual spinach).
- Beetroot.
- Broad beans (latest planted).
- Calabrese.
- French beans.
- Runner beans.
- Cabbage.
- Carrots.
- Cauliflower.
- Celery.
- Courgettes.
- Cucumbers (ridge and greenhouse).
- Globe artichokes.
- Kale.
- Kohlrabi.
- Lettuce.
- Marrows.
- Onions.
- Spring onions.
- Peas.
- Peppers.
- Early maincrop potatoes.
- Radish.
- Spinach.
- Squash (summer custard types).
- Sweetcorn (towards the end of the month if lucky).
- Tomatoes.
- Turnips.

September

Fig. 34. September.

September is the end of summer and, although we're often lucky to have an Indian summer with blue skies and sunshine, nothing is certain with the weather. Whatever the weather brings, September is the month where the season begins to wind down. The bulk of the harvest comes home now and, as crops come out, the plot begins to empty.

There's not a lot to sow but you can be getting hardy winter lettuces in along with spring onions. The most popular spring onion is White Lisbon and it is important to look for the words 'winter hardy' on the packet as ordinary White Lisbon will not go through a harsh period. Plant out your spring cabbage plants to be there for next year and that's about it, except for overwintering onion sets and possibly some winter spinach. The onion sets can be planted through September and into early October to provide a slightly earlier crop than spring-planted sets or onion seed sown under glass in late winter.

That doesn't mean there is nothing to do in the vegetable garden. Your hoe should be continuing to kill the weeds before they establish for starters. You need to be keeping a close eye on the greenhouse crops. The pests are still about enjoying the shelter and you need to watch out for fungal diseases if the weather is not so good and the vents are shut. Leaving the door open in the day to ensure a good airing will sort that.

Tomatoes, peppers, aubergines and cucumbers will continue to need feeding, the rule being not to stop until the fruit has ceased to develop. Outdoor tomatoes and cucumbers will benefit from shelter, unless the weather is exceptionally nice. With bush tomatoes, like plum Roma and San Marzano, the fruits will be ripening but this is attracting the pests. Anti-slug measures are vital; whether you use traps or pellets you need to keep them off.

If you can obtain some straw, this will serve to keep the tomatoes off the soil. Remove any foliage that is yellow, since more air and sun will encourage ripening and the dying leaves just encourage slugs.

On the subject of pests, double check brassicas for cater-pillars. You may be convinced no eggs escaped your attention but they do seem to appear from nowhere at times.

The second early potatoes should be up by now – if not, get them up – and the maincrop potatoes will be ready. The haulm, as we call potato foliage, may well be dying back and will no longer be supplying food to grow the tubers so they're not going to continue growing.

If blight hasn't struck it down, removing the haulm will stop it from starting and being there to infect the crop at the last minute. Late maincrop varieties may still be in full growth and you'll need to watch out for blight on them.

Once the potato crop is cleared, leave for a few days then fork over the top 20cm (8 inches), which will reward you with potatoes that you will be amazed you missed when you harvested. Break up the soil and level out before sowing a green manure like mustard.

As land becomes vacant, this is the time to sow green manures: fast-growing ones to add extra humus when you dig over later in the year; and longer lasting ones where you do not need to dig over to hold nutrients; or sow with legumes such as winter tares to actually add nutrition by fixing nitrogen from the air.

If you have club-root on the plot and can't sow mustard

after your potatoes, try Crimson Clover. It fixes nitrogen and is fast growing if not as prolific as mustard but is easy to dig in. The seeds are very small and 50g will well cover 10 square metres so an even distribution is difficult. The way to get around this is to mix the seeds with bonemeal, which can be bought cheaply and will just slowly release nitrogen. Take an old mixing bowl or similar, add 250g of bonemeal, 50g of seed and mix well. Then sow at 30g per square metre. A set of diet scales is very useful in the potting shed for tasks like this but, if you borrow from the kitchen, do wash them before returning!

Sweetcorn should be ready now, if not in August. The recommended method of testing for ripeness is that you peel back some leaves and press a fingernail into the kernel to see. If the juice runs milky, it is ready. The problem is that you've now opened the cob up to pests, especially pigeons, and you can never get the leaves back properly. As you quickly get a feel for when a cob is ready by looking at its shape and the feel when you squeeze it, don't worry too much about whether it's ripe. It is better to harvest slightly under-ripe rather than over-ripe. Under-ripe is edible but over-ripe becomes hard and tough.

Sweetcorn tends to all come together in a fairly short period and it isn't something you can sow successionally or sow different varieties near to each other to extend the season as they cross pollinate and you can end up with poor cobs across the board. This flush of cobs cannot be avoided but they will keep well in the salad drawer of a fridge, left in the leaves, for up to a week. Otherwise you can blanch (4 minutes for small and 8 minutes for large), and freeze whole to enjoy the taste of summer over the year.

To blanch for freezing, just bring a large pan of water to a rolling boil, put a couple of cobs into the water and time from when the water returns to the boil. Remove from the boiling water and plunge into iced water to cool them quickly and stop the cooking process before freezing.

The sweetcorn generates a load for the compost heap what with the leaves, sweetcorn husks and the stalks. If you don't have a shredder for the stalks, cut into 60cm (2 feet) lengths, lay them on solid ground and bash with a hammer or stamp on them. Then use them at the base of a new compost heap because this month and October are when you will generate the most material for your heaps. Crushing the stems will help them rot but if you don't do this they will decompose eventually.

You may well have reasonably sized parsnips now but they will stay perfectly happy in the ground and do taste better after they have had a frost on them.

The runner beans and French beans will be continuing to produce and the last of the peas should be coming in. Compost the foliage of the peas but leave the roots in the ground as the nodules on them contain nitrogen.

The last of the onions should be drying now. Once harvested, you need to ensure they have dried off to prevent rot in storage. They do best on a rack outdoors, allowing air to blow through, but you need to keep the rain off in some way without laying sheeting directly on them. Drying off in a greenhouse on slatted shelving can work but a sunny day which raises the temperature results in half cooked onions that will definitely rot in store.

Small leeks may well be ready to pull in September. Pull alternates from the row, allowing more space around those left to go through the winter.

Squashes and pumpkins may be ripening now. Try to raise them off the ground for the end run at least to stop rotting. There is nothing more disappointing than lifting a wonderful looking pumpkin to discover that the base is a soggy rotting mess. Large pumpkins can be raised slightly and an old pallet slipped under.

Once the foliage dies back or the squash or pumpkin turns colour, cut the stalk a few centimetres from the fruit and place them in a sunny spot to continue hardening off.

Your maincrop carrots will be ready for lifting some time this month or next. Take off the foliage and store perfect specimens in damp sand in a box in a cool, dark place to last until next year when the early new crop is available. Damaged carrots, nibbled by slugs, can have the bad bits cut off and be frozen in battens.

In addition to the above, you should have the following available:

- Beet leaf (chards and perpetual spinach).
- Beetroot.
- Cabbage.
- Calabrese.
- Carrots.
- Cauliflowers.
- Celery.
- Courgettes.
- Cucumbers.
- Globe artichokes.
- Kohlrabi.
- Leeks (possibly towards the end of the month).
- Lettuce.
- Marrows.
- Peas (last of the crop early in the month).
- Radishes.
- Spring onions.
- Spinach.
- Tomatoes.
- Turnips.

From the greenhouse you should be picking aubergines, chilli and sweet peppers as well as cucumbers and tomatoes.

October

Fig. 35.   October.

By now the weather is cooling fast and the first frosts will probably hit this month so we move from the growing season of one year to the preparation for the next season.

Even the late maincrop potatoes will be coming out of the ground now to store away. After the middle of the month it is probably not worth trying any green manure crops, except the field bean which can be sown as late as early November.

When you harvest potatoes, you are bound to find some that have not been covered when you earthed up, and these will have gone green where exposed to the light. The green potato contains a poisonous alkaloid, solanine, which can cause stomach upsets if eaten. As a rule of thumb, dispose of potatoes that are more than a third green but, if otherwise perfect, store them in complete darkness and in a month or so they will no longer be green.

It's not too late to plant out overwintering onion sets. These are hardy and will overwinter, producing a crop, in theory, about a month earlier than the spring-planted onions. A cloche or fleece covering will get them off to a good start and will stop the birds from pulling them out.

You can plant your garlic now, although this job will hold over into November easily. If you have time and the weather is fine, it's worth doing it when you can because who knows what November's weather will be like.

Towards the end of the month, you can sow broad beans for the earliest crop, all being well. It's always more of a risk sowing at this time of year because in wet soil they may just rot rather than geminate. Always sow a few spares in pots to fill in gaps in the row. If you are in a cold area or have a particularly wet and heavy soil, it is probably not worth winter sowing, especially if you cannot provide cloches to cover them.

Remove any yellowing leaves from overwintering brassicas; they are of no use to the plant and will encourage botrytis to develop and slugs.

The greenhouse will basically finish this month. Remember that peppers, both chilli and sweet, that start green and then turn colour, can taste just as sweet or hot in their green state and may as well come out.

Small under-developed tomatoes are not going to amount to anything and may as well go onto the compost heap with the rest of the plant. Larger green tomatoes, however, are usable immediately in chutneys and pickles or can be ripened over the next few months to provide red tomatoes for eating up to Christmas.

Store them in a cool place in the dark, together but not touching in case one goes to rot and passes it on to the others. A drawer in an unheated bedroom is ideal. Check weekly and remove the ripened ones to eat. If they don't seem to be ripening up, put a ripe or, better still, over-ripe banana in with them which will release ethylene gas that encourages ripening.

The runner beans will certainly finish this month, as will any French beans. Where you've allowed the bean to develop in the pod, these should be dried out.

Spread the pods on the bench in the greenhouse to finish drying and then remove the beans from the shell. These can then be spread on a tray in a warm airy place for a few days to finish drying before storing in air-tight jars for use in winter soups and stews.

When the beans come off, cut the foliage at the base for the compost heap and leave the roots with their nitrogen store in the ground to release in the next year.

Cabbages can come up now too. They'll keep remarkably well in that frost-free shed but beware the slug that may be lurking under the leaves. Sprinkling the outside with salt will deter them from eating away through the winter.

As ground becomes vacant, you can dig it over and spread manure over the surface. Leave the soil roughly dug in large clumps and the worms will break these up as they get the manure. The freezing and thawing of water in the soil will cause the soil to break up finely so becoming easier to handle in the spring.

October and November are good months to undertake double digging, incorporating manure into the bottom of the trench and so deepening your topsoil. If you have access to leaves in bulk from a road sweeper, then add these to the bottom of the trench as well. Thirty centimetres (12 inches) of compressed leaves will go down into a 5cm (2 inch) layer by spring so don't worry if the soil seems very high to start with.

With lighter soils you can place a mulch of leaves about 10cm (4 inches) thick on the surface, weighted down with a light scattering of soil to stop them blowing around. The worms will be kept busy shredding them and dragging them under, improving your soil for you.

However, this is not a good idea on heavy soils as it will just serve to hold water in the soil, making cultivation more difficult in the spring. The retained water will drive the worms away as well, so they aren't there to help.

If you don't have a cage for your leafmould and want to make it, get started at the beginning of the month to be ready when they arrive. If you have one of the combined vacuum shredders that sucks the leaves up and shreds them into a bag, then your leafmould will be ready in late spring. It's worthwhile being a good neighbour and clearing their leaves if they don't want them because leafmould is a fantastic soil conditioner.

If you've not already done so, now's the time for a good clean-out of the greenhouse whilst it is empty. Take out all those pots and bits you've left in there and put them in the shed – you can tidy that up later!

Next, it's time to wash the greenhouse down, using a scrubbing brush and a little detergent and disinfectant or Jeyes fluid. Getting the glass clean will allow more light through in the darker days and cleaning the frame will remove pests who are looking for a good spot to spend the winter.

If you are going to be using the greenhouse through the winter, you can now insulate it. Bubble wrap is good and will do the job. Don't forget you will still need some ventilation or mould will run riot in the house.

You can also get a last sowing of hardy lettuce like Arctic King and grow them on in your greenhouse border to give you a salad whatever the weather.

November

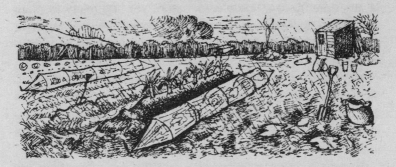

Fig. 36. November.

By now the nights are drawing in, so trying to fit in the gardening work becomes more difficult but the good news is that there is not so much to do at this time of year.

The garlic should go in now to get off to a good start early in the spring but, if you miss sowing it this month, you can sow it in early spring although it likes a cold spell.

Early November is the time for the hardy broad beans like Aquadulce to go in, if you missed this job in October. Sowing winter salads under cover can continue but the germination rates are not good at this time of year. Since the vents are closed in the greenhouse, the atmosphere can become quite stale, encouraging fungal growth, so leave the door and vents open on fine days to give it a good airing.

It's too late for most green manure crops, except possibly for grazing rye, to hold nutrients in the soil for the spring, when it will be dug in. But it's worth a try in a good year.

As with October, as ground becomes vacant, you carry on with the digging over. Although digging over is a pleasant job on a cold day because it keeps you warm, avoid digging over when the ground is frozen and certainly when it is wet and sticking to your boots. Apart from it being much harder work, your standing on the soil is puddling the soil, especially clays.

After digging over, you can apply lime or manure as required, but not both at the same time. Lime can be applied at any time up to a few weeks before you are ready to plant but is best applied to clay soils as soon as they are dug over since the effect of making the clay less sticky will be amplified.

Most of the crops should be in store, except for those left in the ground like the parsnips and Jerusalem artichokes. You can harvest these now if you wish (with the parsnips sweetened by the frosts), or leave them in the ground until you're ready.

Harvest winter cabbages and cauliflowers when they are ready. Cauliflowers will store well in a fridge for a couple of weeks if tightly wrapped with cling film to exclude air. Sticking with the brassicas, the Brussels sprouts should be starting. You are allowed to eat them on other days as well as Christmas Day!

Leeks should be ready; just take what you need and leave the rest to stand until required. You could still be harvesting celery and celeriac, kale and kohlrabi, as well as turnips, swedes and spinach.

If you've grown salsify and scorzonera, these can start to come up late in the month. Salsify is often called the 'vegetable oyster' and, properly cooked, is a wonderful vegetable.

It's worth checking any vegetables you have in store and removing anything that has started to rot before it spreads. Potatoes especially need to be checked and watch out for slugs that have emerged from one potato to go and damage another one.

Continue adding leaves as they fall to your leafmould bin, or bag them to rot down for a year in a shady spot under a hedge. If you have any comfrey still (it dies back in the winter), you can layer it with leaves to create a base for your own potting composts. With the easy and cheap availability of commercial composts nowadays, it is unusual to make your own but adding your leafmould will bulk out commercial composts and the potash added by comfrey is well liked by the bean tribe.

Finally, do check your netting on brassicas. Those pigeons are still keeping a look-out for a winter meal!

December

Fig. 37. December.

The dark days of December are both the end of one year and the start of the new. As the winter solstice (the shortest day of the year) passes, the days again begin to grow longer. It is time to finish one set of tasks and prepare for the next.

Although the December solstice is the start of winter, the coldest weather is yet to come. That honour usually belongs to February so we can still get out into the garden before bad weather stops play. In the ideal world, the efficient gardener will have completed his jobs outdoors and can look forward to sitting with the seed catalogues, his diary and plan his sowings for next year. The rest of us who are merely mortal may have a little more to do!

It is the traditional month for ordering seeds but, before doing so, check what you have left over from the year before. When you buy seeds in the UK they will have a 'use by' date on the packet. Often they will be in a sealed foil packet within the main packet. This excludes air and light which keeps the seed fresh.

Many seeds are supplied in quantities way beyond that required for the average garden or allotment for one year so carefully re-seal the packets, pop them into an airtight box (a Tupperware container is ideal) and store in a cool, dark place. The bottom drawer of a fridge is ideal if you are allowed.

How long your seeds will last when the packet is opened will vary according to the seed, storage conditions and how near the end of its life the seed was when packed. The table opposite is a guide, subject to the caveats above.

Seed	Life in Years
Bean, Broad	2
Bean, French	2
Bean, Runner	2
Beet	5
Beet Spinach	5
Broccoli	5
Cabbage	5
Carrot	3
Cauliflower	5
Cucumber	7
Kale	4
Kohlrabi	4
Leek	3
Lettuce	4
Marrow	6
Courgette	6
Onion	4
Parsley	2
Parsnip	1
Peas	2
Radish	4
Salsify	2
Spinach	2
Swede	2
Tomato	3
Turnip	2

You can test seeds before sowing to check their germination rate. Just place a piece of damp kitchen paper in the bottom of an airtight container and scatter some seeds on it. Place another sheet of damp paper on the top, put the lid on and store in a dark place at room or germination temperature. Check to see which seeds shoot and compare that with the number which don't. That will give you the germination rate. If none develops, then you know they're dead.

After listing what seeds you already have available, you can go on to order your stocks for the new season.

There's nothing to sow in December unless you wish to try some onions from seed in a greenhouse or coldframes – but only if you can ensure they will be kept frost-free. It's almost a tradition with some growers to start their onions off after the Christmas lunch! I would suggest they are fine left for later.

If you have bought your early potatoes, start pushing the chitting process now in a cool room without too much direct sunlight with a view to an early planting of a few tubers in a coldframe, polytunnel or greenhouse. An unused, unheated bedroom is ideal, especially a north-facing one. Do ensure that sheds, etc., are frost-free or the frost will kill the growth off.

General Jobs for December

Digging over can continue, when weather allows. Particularly with clay soils, digging when the soil is wet and sticky can do more harm than good. It's also harder work. As a rule, if your boots become heavy with soil sticking to them it's too wet to dig.

Stake any young trees and tall brassicas to prevent wind rock damaging them by loosening the soil around their roots.

Ensure compost bins are covered to prevent excess rain leaching the nutrients and to keep some of the heat of decomposition in. If you find yourself with time, empty the compost bin and re-build it, out to in and top to bottom, ensuring it's damp but not too wet. This will ensure it rots down evenly, hopefully ready for use in the spring.

Leaves should still be falling so keep adding them to your leafmould pile, creating your future humus.

You can still plant your garlic cloves now. They actually benefit from a period of cold, which prompts growth later. They don't like to sit in water, so if your soil is heavy and holds water, try dibbing a hole with an old spade handle or suchlike. Put about an inch of sand into the base and plant the clove on top, filling above with fine compost. This ensures good drainage and stops them rotting.

Remember that the pigeons will be on the look-out for food, so check the nets on your brassicas to keep them away. It's worth removing any yellow leaves from your winter brassicas – they are doing no good and only encourage diseases such as botrytis. Protect any heads of cauliflower and broccoli by bending over the outer leaves. Any crops in cloches or coldframes will need extra protection if the weather does turn severe. Cover with fleece, sacking, even old net curtains to provide that little extra protection that keeps them alive.

In the greenhouse, if it is kept frost-free, you can continue successional sowings of winter salads. Ventilate the house on warmer days to prevent moulds from becoming established.

December is a good month to go through the shed. Check over your tools, repairing or replacing as need be, and check your machinery. If you have a Rotavator, now is a good time to service it or send it to your local garden machinery specialist before the spring rush starts. You may even get a better price!

What you could be eating now
Leeks are available; just take what you need and leave the rest to stand until required. Leeks are much better harvested from the garden as they are required but in severe weather this can be difficult, so you can lift a few and heel them in on well dug ground; this will not freeze solid.

Just make a shallow trench with one side vertical and the other sloping. Lay the leeks in the trench, roots down and stalk on the sloping side and fill the trench. This provides shelter and keeps the plant alive until required but easy to remove in the worst of weathers.

The carrots should come up for storage now if they haven't already. Store them either in peat or sand or even in a traditional clamp.

Lift celery, parsnips and swedes, although parsnips and swedes are very hardy and may be left if the ground is not needed. You can always cover them with fleece or straw to help stop the ground freezing them in.

Jerusalem artichokes will be available and you can enjoy the salsify and scorzonera.

It's worth another check on any vegetables you have in store and removing anything that has started to rot before it spreads.

Winter cabbages and cauliflowers should be available. Sticking with the brassicas, the Brussels sprouts should be in full production. Just pick from the base of the plant, leaving the smaller sprouts to continue developing at the top of the plant. If sprouts have blown at the base, removing them will help the ones above remain firm.

Other crops you may have available for harvest:

Perpetual spinach, celeriac, chicory (non-forcing and forcing varieties), endive, kale, kohlrabi, lettuce, winter radish, spinach and turnips.

12

BRIEF GUIDE TO
THE VEGETABLES

Introduction

It is not my intention to provide absolute planting instructions
for each and every crop because spacing and timing will vary
for different varieties and growing methods. For example, full
sized cauliflowers in the ground will need 60cm (2 feet)
spacing between plants but a variety bred for close spacing
could be planted in a raised bed just 15cm (6 inches) apart.

Various reference works provide detailed guidance crop by
crop but the information supplied by the reputable seed
merchant on the packet will usually be sufficient and, more
importantly, tailored for the variety supplied.

The problem with suggesting specific varieties is that these
can change over time as improved varieties are developed,
especially now the emphasis is on disease resistance due to the
lack of chemical controls available and the popularity of
organic growing so I have generally tried to avoid this.
Settling down with a few seed catalogues will quickly bring
you up to speed on what is available. As I mentioned when
discussing planning the year, varieties with the RHS award of
garden merit are always a safe bet if you are in doubt.

Asparagus

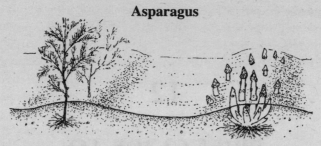

Fig. 38. Asparagus.

Growing asparagus is a long-term project, slow to produce, expensive to start but really worthwhile when you harvest this delicious crop. It takes at least two years to come into production but then will continue for up to 20 years, repaying the initial investment many times over.

In the past it was recommended to grow them on a mounded bed but nowadays a raised deep bed is considered the best method. The roots will go down as far as 1.2 metres (4 feet) so a good depth of soil helps. It needs well drained soil but can be grown on heavier clays that have been well cultivated initially, contain plenty of humus and possibly some grit or sharp sand to open them up.

You can start asparagus from seed but it is more usual to buy one-year-old crowns. These are planted 30–45cm (12–18 inches) apart in April in a 30cm (12 inch) wide trench about 20cm (8 inches) deep, slightly mounded in the centre so the roots slope downwards and out. In a standard raised bed, 1.2 metres (4 feet) wide, the trench goes down the centre. Cover with fine riddled (sieved) soil to about 5cm (2 inches) above the top of the crown and then fill to the surface as the plant grows.

Asparagus plants are either male or female. The male plants are more productive and all male F1 hybrids are available, with their energies going into edible spears rather than berries.

Keep the bed weed-free, water as required but avoid it being too wet and do not take a crop in the first year. The plants are shallow so be careful if hoeing not to go deep; it's best to hand-weed in a raised bed. The spears turn into foliage to feed the plant. In autumn, the fern-like foliage begins to yellow and should be cut off about 5–10cm (2–4 inches) above ground level.

In the spring, draw up a ridge over the plant centre about 10cm (4 inches) high and add a balanced fertilizer like fish, blood and bone or Growmore. The spears start to appear in early May and there is no point in telling you not to take any, so just take a few, leaving the rest to develop,

Cut the spears with a sharp knife some 7.5cm (3 inches) below the ground when they are about 10cm (4 inches) high above the ground. The real season starts in mid-May and runs through June when you must show restraint and stop cutting. In the second year just take 6 or 8 spears per plant, double that in the third year and expect about 20–25 spears per plant for the next 20 years.

If a late frost strikes in May, it will damage the crop so cover with fleece. Otherwise your main pest will be slugs, although rust can be a problem in wet years. Remove affected shoots if rust strikes. The asparagus beetle is rarely a problem to home growers. They are small with orange markings on their 7mm-long bodies and will attack foliage and spears. Use an approved insecticide such as Derris.

The main problem with asparagus is over cropping in the early years causing weakened plants and spindly spears. It is hard, but restraint will pay you back.

Aubergine

Fig. 39. Aubergine.

The aubergine or egg plant is very much a staple of Mediterranean cuisine, best known as the main ingredient in Moussaka but actually quite versatile and now becoming more popular in Britain. The fruit can be exceptionally attractive, jet black with a deep shine. The stems are a little prickly so using gloves is a sensible precaution.

It really is a greenhouse crop. Growing out of doors is unlikely to succeed even in the south unless the summer is exceptional. The best known varieties are the large black ones but white and red aubergines can be had with size varying from hen's egg size up to 500g for large ones.

Seeds are sown in late February or early March in a heated propagator or window sill then potted along until being planted either in the border, growbags or in 20/25cm (8/10 inch) pots. The plants usually need staking, especially as the weight of fruit can break the stems. Mist spraying when the flowers have formed will encourage fruit set. Limit to four or five fruits with standard varieties to ensure good weight and stop the stem by pinching out at 30cm (12 inches). Feed in exactly the same way as tomatoes with proprietary tomato food or with comfrey tea.

Aubergines are usually easy enough to cultivate but they do seem to attract whitefly and aphid problems. Another common problem is red spider mite, although they cause only minimal damage. Misting will deter them or you can use an insecticide such as Derris.

Beet Leaf

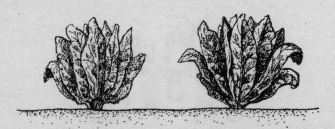

Fig. 40.   Spinach beet.

Fig. 41. Ruby chard.

Fig. 42. Sea kale or silver beet (Swiss chard).

This is one of those confusing vegetables called by more than one name. Swiss chard, ruby chard, spinach beet, sea kale, silver beet and perpetual spinach are all variations of the same vegetable.

True spinach can be tricky to grow, prone to bolting in dry weather but the chards are fairly trouble free. Some of the chards are decorative enough to grace the flower border without looking out of place.

Sow thinly in April in good soil, preferably manured the preceding winter. They will be in the ground for over a year but a small row, perhaps 2 metres (6½ feet) long is all you need.

When they have grown large enough to handle, thin to one plant per 20–30cm (8–12 inches) and keep weed-free and watered in dry weather. Harvesting can start in August and will provide leaves right through to the following June by which time the plants will be getting tired and can come up, freeing the soil for another crop. Move your beet leaf bed round the plot, sowing in a different place each spring.

You don't harvest all the leaves in one go, just take a few outer leaves of each plant, preferably fairly young so cropping the whole row in one go. Be careful not to disturb the roots during this.

They are remarkably trouble free, the only pest to worry about being the slugs.

Beetroot

Fig. 43. Two types of beetroot.
(1) Globe or round.
(2) Oval or long.

The beetroot is a crop that has benefited from the breeder's art and modern varieties are exceptional, being easy to grow and producing consistent results with a little care.

The older varieties of globe beetroot had a tendency to get white rings inside but with modern varieties this just doesn't happen.

Although we think of beetroot being a deep red colour you can actually get yellow and white varieties, despite the usual choice being red.

Beetroot seeds are unusual. They are actually a cluster of seeds in one package so thinning is nearly always required unless pelleted seed is bought. However, some varieties come as monogerms, which means one seed per package.

Bolting can be a problem with the earliest sowings, so for these choose varieties such as Boltardy. The main sowing season starts in late April and runs through to July but you can sow under cloche as early as mid March.

Sow directly 2–3cm (1 inch) deep at a spacing of 10cm (4 inches) in rows 30cm (12 inches) apart, thinning to one plant per station. They are not too fussy about the soil, but you should correct acid soils by liming and ensure a good level of humus for best results.

Once sown it is a matter of keeping the weeds off and ensuring they get sufficient water. Dryness will cause low yields of a woody texture and cracked roots. You can pull alternate roots when they reach the size of a golf ball, leaving the rest to grow on a little.

The later June-sown crops can be left to mature fully for lifting in October and storing as a winter crop in the same way as carrots and parsnips.

Beetroot are generally an easy, trouble-free crop and the bane of older growers, bolting, is not much of a problem with modern bolt-resistant varieties.

Although the globe-shaped beetroot is best known nowadays, there are cylindrical varieties that have the benefit of storing well and they can make the cook's job easier by providing slices of equal diameter.

Long varieties, very much a root crop, are available; these require a deep sandy soil to perform really well. They do produce a larger crop from a given area but they tend to be more popular with exhibitors growing for show than gardeners growing for table.

Brassicas

The cabbage tribe is one of the most important families in the plot including cabbages, kale and cauliflowers, Brussels sprouts, broccoli and calabrese, along with swedes, turnips, radish and mustard. It is said that the good gardener should be able to provide a fresh cauliflower on any day of the year and certainly the cabbage tribe is one staple that will provide something whatever the season.

Because they are, usually, leaf vegetables they require plenty of nitrogen to be available and they all share a love of lime. They also need a constant supply of water which is best served from ground rich in humus.

They are less tolerant than many other crops and meeting these requirements can be difficult but the rewards are there if you succeed.

The ideal brassica bed needs both nitrogen and humus so the addition of manure in autumn will accomplish both. Dig over the soil and then add a barrow load of manure per square metre to the land. You can even add more if you wish, some of the best brassica growers add twice that amount. Leave be for the winter to give the worms a chance to take some down into the soil. In the early spring, fork over the top 15cm (6 inches) to mix the manure in or run over with a Rotavator and leave for a week to settle.

Now adding the manure will have had the effect of making the soil more acid and if any plant does not like an acid soil it is the brassica. If you can do, test the pH to measure the acidity and add the appropriate amount of lime to take the level up to 7.0. If it goes a little higher it will not matter so, if you cannot test, just add about a kilogram per square metre and leave this to weather in for a couple of weeks.

Never add lime and manure at the same time because they react together and neither benefits.

You now have a near perfect brassica bed but they are greedy plants and adding 60g per square metre of a general purpose fertilizer such as Growmore or fish, blood and bone before planting out will benefit them.

Most failures with the cabbage tribe come down to lack of nutrition so if you cannot provide loads of manure, add additional fertilizer. With Brussels sprouts that require a long growing season, an additional boost mid-season will often make a dramatic difference to the final crop. Since they are producing leaves, albeit wrapped up tightly with the sprout, it is nitrogen they are most likely short of. A sprinkling of dried blood or sulphate of ammonia around the base of the plant will do the trick.

If the plants do not seem to be doing well, and the cause is not a disease or pest, then feeding with a high nitrogen liquid fertilizer may well save the day.

The main problems shared by the brassica family are club-root, cabbage root fly, caterpillars and, of course, the slugs and pigeons. Club-root affects the whole range except the salad radish which grows too quickly to notice the club-root. The cabbage root fly also sometimes hits the swedes; covering with a fleece until they are established is the only defence.

Broad Beans

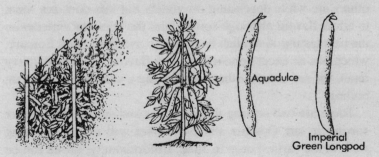

Fig. 44. Broad bean.

The broad bean (fava beans to the Americans) is very under-rated, often with a reputation for being tough and causing wind, which is undeserved for picked young they are tender, sweet and do not cause wind. Older beans can be blanched and rubbed to remove the outer skin, which is somewhat tough and may be the cause of wind.

Like all beans, they are high in protein and fibre so provide a healthy addition to the diet, especially valuable for vegetarians. As a legume they provide their own nitrogen and leave some behind after cropping if the stalks are taken to the compost heap, leaving the roots to decompose in the ground.

They are an easy crop to grow, not requiring too much attention. They like a soil high in humus so ground previously manured is ideal, even though they produce their own nitrogen. They like a lot of potash so if you provide extra it will benefit the crop. A kilogram per square metre of wood ashes, or 40–50g per square metre of sulphate of potash applied a month before sowing or planting will be sufficient. This also prevents a fungal infection called chocolate spot.

The beans come in three main types: longpods (which can be nearly 40cm (16 inches) long with 8–10 beans per pod), Windsor (which are shorter and fatter with 4–7 beans per pod) and dwarf varieties that grow just 30–45cm (12–16 inches) high, half as much as the others. Some beans are green and others are white depending on variety but this does not seem to affect flavour although some claim the Windsor varieties as the best tasting. A reddish bean is also available: Red Epicure, which has an exceptional distinctive flavour. If steamed, they retain the red colour, otherwise turning a yellowish colour on boiling.

There are two sowing times, winter and spring. The winter sowing in late October and November will result, all being well, in the earliest crop in June. Unfortunately, losses can be high, especially in a wet winter with seeds rotting in the ground, even when cloched to start. Some varieties, such as Aquadulce, are more suitable than others for winter sowing although all the broad beans are hardy. In a bad winter or spring it makes little difference to cropping time and the spring sown beans will catch up. These can go in as early as late February under cloche or as late as early May to provide a cropping period from June to October.

Early spring sowings are best made in 8cm (3 inch) pots under glass or in the cool greenhouse for planting out around three weeks later. If sowing direct, it is well to sow a few in pots anyway to plug holes in the row.

The usual garden spacing is 20cm (8 inches) apart in a row with another row 20cm (8 inches) away, staggering the plants so they will provide support to each other. These double rows are spaced 60–75cm (24–30 inches) apart to allow access for picking. In windy areas, it will be necessary to provide support by means of wires strung on the outside of the double rows.

The main problem suffered by broad beans are masses of blackflies on the growing tips in the summer. The simple answer is to snip off the top 15cm (6 inches) of the plant with its squatters and dispose of them.

Broad beans freeze well and can be dried for storage.

Broccoli and Calabrese

Fig. 45. Broccoli.

The supermarkets have helped to confuse the issue of what is broccoli and what is a calabrese by calling both by either name. The simple thing to keep in mind is that broccoli is an overwintered crop but calabrese produces its crop the same year before winter.

Both are brassicas and the general brassica growing instructions apply.

Broccoli
These consist of Purple Sprouting and White Sprouting, with early varieties being ready first. Generally they are sown in

spring, and planted out in early summer for a crop in February/March through to May. The spears are removed from the plants and turn green on cooking. They should be freshly picked for best flavour. The average seed packet contains enough for two hundred plants and the average family would probably need two or three plants but the seeds will store for up to four years.

Because they are standing through the winter, a sheltered site is best and earthing up around the stems to 10cm (4 inches) will help keep the plant stable and prevent wind rock.

Calabrese

The flavour is milder and much preferred by many and is an easier crop to grow. Sow in early spring, under glass, to plant out in June and July to provide a crop from August through October.

With some varieties, cutting off the spears and leaving the plant in the ground will result in a second flush – a free extra crop, albeit smaller than the first.

Romanesco

This is often described as a calabrese but it can be described as a green cauliflower. It is a sort of cross between the two, producing large pyramid-shaped heads with a unique delicate flavour. These are large plants and require a spacing between 75–90cm (30–36 inches).

Spacing and planting times will vary considerably with individual varieties of broccoli and calabrese so check the seed packet carefully.

Brussels Sprouts

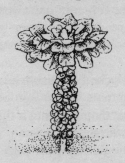

Fig. 46.   Brussels sprouts.

For too many people the Brussels sprout is the vegetable suffered on Christmas Day after being cooked to a recipe of 'boil until ruined'. Cooked properly, they are delicious and they can be enjoyed fresh from September through February.

To cook them, just clean and remove any loose outer leaves then drop into water at a rolling boil for two or three minutes. Remove and drain well, then gently sauté in butter with plenty of black pepper for a few minutes. You will not recognize them as the same soggy vegetable suffered with Christmas lunch.

The sprout packs a lot into a small space. Just completely strip the leaves from one sprout and spread them on a table. You will be surprised how much leaf is crammed in there.

Started off in March and April, they are usually planted out in May and June where they will sit until required, even through to March. Do allow enough space for them, most varieties need 75cm (30 inches) between plants.

Because they are in the ground so long and put so much into each sprout, they really benefit from an extra feed in August or September to produce well.

In early autumn as the sprouts begin to form, drawing some earth a few centimetres up around the stem, or mulching with garden compost, will help stabilize the plant as well. The sprout is a tall plant and will catch the wind. Wind rock moves the roots, breaking the tiny root hairs that take water and food into the plant and so causing lower yields. Planting in a sheltered spot will help stop this and staking tall varieties is worthwhile.

Wind rocking and lack of available nutrients cause the most common fault with sprouts: blown sprouts. This is where they start to open up rather than forming a tight head. The sprouts develop from low on the stem and removing the blown sprouts and feeding with a liquid fertilizer high in nitrogen can stop the problem, allowing the sprouts further up the plant to develop properly.

Sprouts left too long on the plant will blow anyway so removing them is a continual process. Gluts can be frozen, just blanch for two or three minutes beforehand and remember they are effectively three-quarter cooked when you defrost them.

Once you have stripped the sprouts from the plant, the top can be removed and used as cabbage, a bonus crop.

Older varieties often tend to be more susceptible to blowing than the modern F1 hybrid varieties. These F1 varieties have been more developed for the farmer than the garden grower so they produce over a short period which is great for picking in one go to supply the shops for the Christmas rush. For the home grower an extended cropper can be a better bet.

Each plant can produce around a kilogram so limit the number of plants to a sensible level; for an average family six plants will be more than sufficient.

Pest and disease problems are the same as other brassicas but do remember there are few edible crops available for the pigeons in winter, so net them.

Cabbages

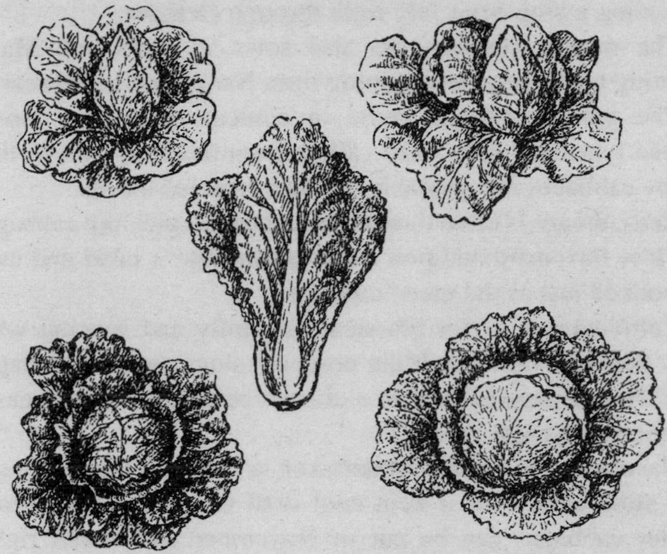

Fig. 47. Different varieties of cabbage.

The humble cabbage suffers from a bad press due to the over-cooked soggy mess that was served up as cabbage to so many of us in our youth. Yet properly cooked it is a delicious vegetable and surprisingly contains nearly twice the vitamin C of an apple or orange and four times that of the potato, making it a very healthy part of our diet.

By choosing the correct varieties, you can arrange to provide fresh cabbage throughout the year. However, avoid the temptation to grow too many. Just twelve cabbages in a year will be sufficient for most families.

The cabbage comes in three waves, spring, summer and winter, with varieties being described by their cutting period not their sowing times.

The spring cabbages are sown in July and August for planting out in September and October to be ready in April and May. The summer cabbages are sown in late winter/early spring – February and March sowings under glass and April outside to be planted out from late April through June, providing a crop from July right through October.

The winter cabbages are also sown in April and May, planting out in July but cropping from November to February.

The green cabbages come in conical, somewhat loose leaved types and tight balls called drum head, as well as the savoy cabbages recognizable by their crinkled leaves.

Red cabbage is often thought of as being a pickling cabbage but it is flavourful addition when grated into a salad and can be cooked just as the green cabbages.

Cultivation is as for brassicas generally and spacing will vary between varieties. Main pests are slugs and the cabbage root fly (see page 114), with club-root being the main disease problem (see page 113).

Harvesting is usually undertaken as needed but cabbage will store quite well if kept cool until required. Drum head winter cabbages can be cut in November and stored right through to spring. Cut off the stem and remove outer leaves where any slugs may be hiding. Keep cool and dark. When you harvest spring and summer cabbages, you can cut the stem about 5cm (2 inches) from the ground and then make a cross in the top, about a centimetre deep, which will result in the plant forming four small heads, giving you a free secondary crop.

Chinese Cabbage

Sometimes sold as 'Chinese leaves' or pak-choi, these cabbages look more like a lettuce than the traditional cabbage. Cultivation is different in that they are sown in place and are not transplanted. Depending on the variety, sowing varies but is usually in July or August, enabling a crop from these fast-growing plants in October. The usual instruction is to sow at 10cm (4 inch) spacing in rows 30cm (12 inches) apart and thin to 30cm (12 inches) apart in the row.

Capsicums

Capsicums is the 'fancy' name for the peppers, which come in two types: the sweet pepper used in salads and cooked dishes and the hot chilli peppers. Both are grown in the same way but the chilli peppers are far less prone to insect damage to the fruit. One wonders why!

It is possible to grow peppers outdoors in a fine summer in the south of England but really they are a greenhouse crop.

Sow under heat in late February and March, moving the seedlings along to 8cm (3 inch) pots when large enough to handle and from there to a 15cm (6 inch) pot, and then plant into their final home. They do well in the border of the greenhouse or in 20–25cm (8–10 inch) pots. Growbags can be used but they do better in pots.

The plants can reach around 90cm (3 feet) high and will usually need tying to a stake because the weight of fruit will overwhelm the plant.

Once the flowers appear it is a good idea to mist spray with water; it encourages the fruit to set and deters the red spider mite. At this point, start feeding just as for tomatoes. When the fruits are the right size for the variety, they are edible and can be taken. All the fruits are green when first formed and coloured varieties change to red or yellow over the next week or so on the plant. The flavour does not change greatly, just the appearance. Coloured sweet peppers will brighten up any meal. Chilli peppers do not get noticeably hotter as they change colour.

The chilli peppers are smaller than their sweet brethren and come in a range of shapes from small globes to 10cm (4 inch) thin tubes. Usually there are a lot of fruit on the chilli plants and one or two plants will provide more than enough. The sweet peppers are less productive in numbers, around 6–10 per plant, although the fruits are larger.

The 'hotness' of the chilli pepper is caused by a chemical called capsaicin and the more of this, the hotter the chilli. The measure of this hotness is made in Scoville units, named after the test's inventor. The hottest pepper ever tested was the Naga Jolokia, an Indian pepper at 1,040,000 Scovilles. The Habanero chillies run around the 100,000 to 350,000 level and the Jalapeno at 2,500 to 8,000. Even a Jalapeno is pretty hot so be aware.

Warning. When preparing chilli peppers, the capsaicin will get onto your fingers. Wash your hands very thoroughly afterwards because touching your eyes or any sensitive place will be exceptionally painful.

Sweet peppers can be stored in the fridge for a week or blanched and frozen. Chilli peppers can be frozen but they are easily stored by tying in open bunches and allowing them to dry.

Like tomatoes, peppers can suffer blossom end rot if they are watered irregularly. Otherwise the main pests are red spider mite and aphids. Effective biological controls for both are available.

Carrots

The carrot, like the pea, is one of our most popular vegetables and it is one of the oldest vegetables eaten by man. The original thin roots were white, purple, red, yellow/green and black – not orange at all, which was a breeding innovation from the Dutch to celebrate the House of Orange.

Nowadays you can again grow carrots in colours apart from orange including a deep purple variety, Healthmaster, which provides 33–35 per cent more beta carotene than any other carrot. Carrots are an excellent source of vitamin A and potassium; they contain vitamin C, vitamin B6, thiamine, folic acid, and magnesium. Unfortunately, they don't really enable you to see in the dark. That idea was brilliant propaganda from the British government in the Second World War to confuse the Germans about the success of radar-guided fighters and to convince the civilians to eat more of an abundant crop.

Carrots come in various shapes as well as colours: small round carrots through short cylindrical ('stump-rooted') to long-rooted varieties more suited to show growers than table growers. Some are fast to develop and designed to be eaten fresh in around 10–12 weeks from sowing whereas others, the maincrop varieties, take around 16 weeks to mature and can be stored for use over the winter.

The most notable early varieties, Amsterdam Forcing and Early Nantes, are ideal for an early planting in a greenhouse border.

The carrot may be popular but it is not the easiest vegetable to grow. The soil must be deep, fertile and free of stones but you should not grow in soil manured the previous winter or the roots will tend to split or fork, producing those convoluted monsters so popular as a novelty item.

A sandy soil is best but if that is not available grow stump-rooted varieties where the root is more of a cylinder than a long cone. It is worthwhile on hard heavy soils growing in a specially constructed raised bed filled with a sand/sieved compost mixture. Add a general purpose fertilizer a couple of weeks before sowing in any case.

There are two ways of growing: the area method, which is ideal for early varieties, and raised beds or in rows in the soil. The area method involves thinly scattering the seed over the surface and dusting with sand to hold the seeds in place. When the seedlings can be handled, thin out to around 2–4cm (1½ inches) apart. After six weeks thin again but this time the thinnings will be large enough to make a tender addition to a salad or cooked with a meal.

Otherwise sow in traditional rows, 15cm (6 inches) between rows and, depending on the variety, around 10cm (4 inches) apart in the row after the final thinning.

The main problem is the carrot root fly as described on page 112. Otherwise cultivation consists of ensuring there is sufficient water and keeping weeds from crowding the crop. With the area method, hoeing is not possible but the density of the foliage should shade out most weeds. In rows be very careful with the hoe; hand-weeding is recommended.

Harvest can be from as early as mid-May from a greenhouse border through to November. Leaving the carrots in the ground after they are mature invites damage from slugs and they are best harvested when ready.

Carrots can be stored in damp sand or peat in a frost-free shed or frozen in battens. Freezing is best where the carrot has some damage as it is unlikely to store otherwise.

If you fancy growing the long carrots like those exhibited in shows, be aware that the record to beat at the time of writing is over 5.14 metres set by Bernard Lavery of Llanherry, South Wales.

Cauliflowers

Fig. 48. Cauliflower.

The cauliflower is not the easiest of the brassica family to grow but a large white cauliflower with tight white curds is a thing of beauty and producing one a source of much satisfaction.

They are very vulnerable to club-root but you can grow ordinary cauliflowers by following the instructions on coping with club-root. Club-root resistant varieties are being bred and the first of these, Clapton, from Thompson and Morgan, is now available. Check the seed catalogues for new varieties.

When starting in modules and moving up through the pots, ensure they do not become pot bound. It's easy enough to check the root system, just turn upside down, allowing the plant to come between your fingers which form a plate to stop the compost from falling out and lift the pot. If the white roots go around and around, then it is pot bound. Move on but tease the roots out so they do not continue the endless circle.

Ensure they are well firmed in and watered when planting out so that the roots establish well in the ground. When planting out or moving up to a large pot, cauliflowers and cabbages should be planted deep, up to the base of the first seed leaves. This helps them have a firm stalk.

If they don't establish good roots because they are circling, or the plant isn't firm which allows it to rock and break those minute root hairs that are where the nutrients come in to the plant, then the effect will be the same as for a soil that lacks nutrients. The plant will form its curds early and a small cauliflower will be the result. In extreme cases these will be golf-ball sized!

We love the taste of the cauliflower and so do the pests. Caterpillars will not only eat the leaves but can get into the curd itself and slugs love to climb the stem to eat away in the sheltered centre, leaving brown trails where they have munched their way across the surface.

More than any other brassica, they are vulnerable to those pests as well as the cabbage root fly.

So to recap: rich firm soil, plant properly and protect against pests for a good result.

I mentioned the tight white curds. If too much sunlight gets onto the head then it will go slightly yellow and off colour. To prevent this, bend some of the inner leaves over the head to shade it. If you leave the cauliflower too long after the head has formed, then the curds continue to grow, coming apart so, once it is ready, harvest. Some varieties will stand longer than others; check in your seed catalogue for varieties described as holding well.

You don't have to grow white cauliflowers either. Recently yellow and purple varieties have become available. The Purple Graffiti variety is particularly striking and retains its colour when cooked. The flavour is not, unfortunately, quite as good as the normal white varieties but it did convince a young man who hated cauliflowers, along with any other vegetable, to eat this 'super space cauliflower'.

It is possible to have a cauliflower to cut nearly every day of the year but usually from March to November. There are three types: summer varieties that can be started in late winter to be ready as early as June or July; autumn varieties for October and November; and the winter varieties that are very slow to mature, taking 40 to even 50 weeks to mature from March through to June.

Celeriac

Fig. 49.   Celeriac.

This is also known as turnip root celery and is more popular in Europe than Britain, probably for good reason. It is a demanding crop, requiring starting in heat in March then being planted out in manure-rich, fertile soil in a sunny spot in late May, spaced 30cm (12 inches) apart in 45cm (18 inch) rows.

As it grows, you need continually to remove side shoots to expose the crown and then earth up in September. All the while you must keep the crop weed-free and regularly watered, taking precautions against slugs and carrot fly.

In November you harvest a white, knobbly ball about 10–12cm (4½ inches) in diameter for all this trouble, which, when thickly peeled, can be grated into salads or cubed for use in stews where it adds a celery-like flavour. They can be left in the ground and lifted as required or stored as other root crops like carrots and parsnips.

You may feel it is a lot of trouble for a poor result, especially if you do not particularly like celery but tastes do vary.

Celery

Fig. 50. Celery.

Growing celery used to be the real test of a gardener's skill, requiring special trenching and two people, one to hold the leaves together and one to shovel soil to blanch the celery. Modern self-blanching varieties are still demanding but far easier than that.

Sow in heat under glass in late March to early April and ensure they are never checked (stopped from growing) by drops in temperature, carefully hardening off for a planting in late May to early June.

The soil needs to be really good, incorporating plenty of manure and compost, as celery is a really greedy crop. A week before planting add a general purpose fertilizer such as Growmore or fish, blood and bone. Planting is usually in a block around 20cm (8 inches) between plants so they cover each other but inserting straw between plants may be needed to help the blanching process and wrapping of the outer plants in the block.

These self-blanching varieties are less stringy and finer flavoured than the old trenching varieties but are not hardy so will be finished when the hard winter frosts arrive.

The biggest problem is the slug which seems to have a special affection for celery. Damage by slugs can also cause a bacterial disease, celery heart rot, to take hold ruining the plant as it turns the centre to a brown slimy mess.

Bolting is another problem. It is critical that the plants not be allowed to dry out in good weather, so water daily in hot spells.

Chicory

Fig. 51.   Chicory.

Chicory is one crop that you either love or hate the taste of, worth thinking about before you grow it! It makes a great addition to a winter salad, if you like its astringent flavour, or it can be eaten as a cooked vegetable.

There are two types: forcing and non-forcing. The non-forcing are easiest and earlier but the forcing varieties have a finer flavour. The non-forcing varieties are sown thinly in rows 30cm (12 inches) apart and thinned down to 30cm (12 inches) apart in the row. Harvest in November and December for immediate use, although they will store in a cool dark shed for a while. If a hard frost threatens, provide some protection.

The forcing varieties are more complex. Sow a little earlier in May than non-forcing types and thin down to 15cm (6 inches) apart. In November dig up the plants with the roots. Discard any where the root's crown is less than 2.5cm (1 inch) across, the roots are damaged or forked. Cut the foliage off a couple of centimetres above the crown and trim back the root to around 15cm (6 inches) in length. Store in damp sand in a cool dark place.

When you want to produce a crop, plant five roots into damp multi-purpose compost in a 25cm (10 inch) pot. Place another pot over the top to exclude light and keep in a room at 13–15° Celsius and the blanched chicons will grow.

Some florists and supermarkets will sell off the pots, in which cut flowers are delivered and sold, for pennies. These are ideal for chicory, being about the right size and black in colour. Drill holes in the pot for drainage but not in the cover. These also make ideal pots for peppers and tomatoes, yet cost nothing compared to buying a large pot.

Although forcing chicory is a fussy business, if you like shop-bought forced chicons you will find doing this at home worthwhile because they are fresher and have not been exposed to the light at all, avoiding the bitterness that develops with shop-bought ones.

Courgettes and Marrows

Fig. 52.   Courgettes.

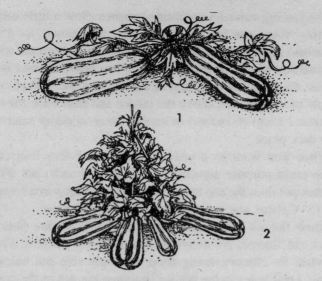

Fig. 53. Marrow.
(1) A trailing marrow.
(2) A bush marrow.

Courgettes and marrows are cucurbits like the squashes and pumpkins so their growing requirements are much the same. Follow the instructions for pumpkins, spacing at 60cm (2 feet) apart each way.

A courgette is just an immature marrow and if you leave a courgette on the plant it will grow on to become a marrow. Having said that, different varieties have been developed for each and so usually just leaving a courgette to develop will produce a very inferior marrow.

Courgettes are best harvested small – cylindrical varieties when they are around 10cm (4 inches) long. You can even cook the flowers in batter if you wish. As well as the standard green courgette, yellow varieties are available and ball shaped instead of the cylinder shape.

Regular picking will keep the plant cropping, and sheltering with large cloches at the end can extend the season, giving fruit from June right through October.

Courgettes can fail to set fruit in poor weather when pollinating insects may not be about but F1 hybrids are available that will set fruit without pollination. The temptation is to sow the entire packet of seeds, which tend to have a good germination rate. Two plants will be sufficient for the average family, probably more than sufficient, so sow four seeds and discard the weaker two. If you are trying a number of varieties, then one plant of each will be enough. Start two plants though to provide a reserve in case of failure. The seeds have a life expectancy of six years so save the rest of the packet for the following year and the ones after.

Marrows are cultivated in exactly the same way except the fruits are left to develop and are limited to a maximum of four fruits per plant. Like squashes, the skins are allowed to harden at the end of the season and a marrow will store well for a few months. Treat as a squash.

Unlike the courgette, the marrow's skin is not eaten, being too tough and the seeds are removed. As well as in the traditional stuffed marrow dishes, they are useful in chutneys and, with their mild flavour, as a bulking agent in jams.

Apart from slugs, marrows and courgettes are usually trouble free although they are susceptible to cucumber mosaic virus. (Cucumbers are also cucurbits.) You can buy varieties with resistance to this.

Cucumbers

Fig. 54.   Cucumber (outdoor ridge type).

Cucumbers are one of those vegetables where the difference between shop-bought tasteless tubes of water and home grown is most noticeable. They are grown outside or in the greenhouse and the greenhouse cucumber is actually the more difficult to grow, despite a controlled environment and arguably it is inferior in flavour.

The greenhouse varieties crop earlier than outdoor varieties, but to get that earlier crop you need to be able to maintain temperature if a late cold spell arrives. It used to be that you needed to remove male flowers from the greenhouse cucumbers to avoid a bitter flavour in the fruits but the breeders came through again with all-female F1 hybrids saving that chore. However, the all-female varieties tend to need a warmer greenhouse to perform well.

Started in mid-March, they are planted either into the greenhouse border, large pots or growbags when large enough and will commence fruit production in June, usually running through the summer until October. Sow the flat seeds sideways on so water doesn't sit on the seed, to prevent rotting, directly into an 8cm (3 inch) pot of multi-purpose compost in a propagator or indoors, allowing the temperature to fall gradually when taken out.

They don't like changes in temperature (a cold night can really check production) and they don't like having the base of the stem wet, which can rot. To get around this, water through a lemonade bottle sunk into the border or, when growing in growbags, insert a bottomless pot into the bag just to water through.

The cucumber is a climbing plant so you will need to provide canes for them to cling too. However, be aware there will be a fair weight so ensure the canes are going to be stable and strong.

Cucumbers are susceptible to cucumber mosaic virus, which is passed by aphids, so controlling greenfly is quite important. Feeding is important too. Treat as tomatoes and feed when the fruits have begun forming.

The greenhouse cucumber may arrive earlier but the outdoor or ridge cucumber usually wins out for flavour. They often have a spiky skin and are shorter and fatter than the greenhouse varieties, so they need to be peeled before eating.

Prepare the ground for them by filling a 30cm (12 inch) deep and square hole with a good rich compost to feed the plant through the season. Leave the top slightly mounded and either directly sow two or three seeds into the mound or start in pots indoors and plant out later. If you can keep the plant covered with a cloche, it will help it get off to a good start; even a cut-down bottle over the seedling to start will make a difference.

Inserting a cut-down bottle into the mound to water through will be helpful. Although ridge cucumbers are not as delicate as greenhouse types, they don't like wet stems too much either.

When the leading stem has developed eight leaves, pinch out the growing tip, and side shoots will develop, bearing extra fruits. You can just leave the shoots to trail along the ground but the cucumbers on the ground are very vulnerable to rotting and slug damage. Slugs are the prime pest with outdoor cucumbers and you really need to take action against them.

Lifting the shoots and eventual fruits off the ground by providing a frame of some sort is worthwhile. On an allotment, training the plant over an old pallet is sufficient or you can fix some wire netting to wooden laths and support this on upturned pots.

The breeders have developed all-female varieties of ridge cucumbers as well. You do not remove male flowers from the standard varieties but they do form seeds in the fruit but not in the all-female varieties.

Japanese varieties are generally very good and these can be trained up a strong vertical frame. Burpless Tasty Green is one of these and certainly has an exceptional flavour.

For both greenhouse and ridge cucumbers, harvest the first

fruits small to encourage the plant to keep producing, Do not leave developed fruits on the plant to go yellow because it will cease production. The fruits are cut off the stem with a knife or secateurs; do not pull them away or you will damage the plant or fruit.

Cucumber tends to be a glut crop, one or two plants being sufficient for the average family but often fruits arrive like buses, in a bunch. They will keep for a while in the fridge but you cannot freeze them. One storage method available is to salt them.

French Beans

Fig. 55.   Dwarf French bean plant in crop.

French beans are considered something of a gourmet crop but they are very easy to grow. Most are best eaten as pods but some are best for allowing the bean to develop as haricots. There are many varieties available: flat pods, pencil pods in shape, and yellow- and purple-coloured pods, as well as the more usual green ones. The yellow waxy pod varieties have a particularly good flavour but do not tend to freeze well, unfortunately, unlike the green pod types.

As with all the bean family, they produce their own nitrogen but they like humus in the soil and will benefit from additional potash. Sowing is usually direct and can be started under cloche in late March, early April, although they are not hardy and better results will come from a May sowing. You must protect from late frosts. Generally they are sown 5cm (2 inches) deep, 10cm (4 inches) apart in rows 45cm (18 inches) apart. Another method, favoured in France, is to sow in pockets of 5–8 seeds spaced some 50cm (20 inches) apart equidistantly.

Cropping can start as early as July and with successional sowing through to the first frosts in October. Picking continually encourages the formation of a another flush, and feeding with a tomato type of liquid fertilizer will keep production going.

Where you are growing for haricots (dried beans), just leave the pods on the plant to swell and the pods begin to dry. Remove the pods and hang indoors to dry until the pods are brittle and begin to split. Shell the beans and dry further on a rack then store in an airtight container. You can uproot the entire plant and hang this upside down to dry rather than hang individual pods if you prefer.

The most popular variety of haricot is the Borlotti bean which is also available as a climbing bean. The climbing varieties are extremely productive for the small area they cover. They're not quite as attractive as runner beans, although the red and yellow pods are very attractive, but they would still make a good backdrop in a flower border.

Treat in a similar way to runner beans, providing canes for support. The dwarf varieties usually do not require much or any support. If they do need it, use short twigs or pea sticks to stop the plants toppling over.

Garlic

Fig. 56. Garlic.

There was a time where garlic was viewed with dark suspicion in Britain but now it is almost as popular as in the Mediterranean countries. Luckily for us it is easy to grow, even in our slightly cooler climate.

It comes in two types: hard neck and soft neck. The hard-neck varieties do not store as well as the soft-necked types, which can be platted into strings to hang in the shed until required but some people prefer the flavour of the hard-neck varieties.

Do not just buy a garlic bulb in the supermarket to plant out. It is going to be a foreign variety, bred for warmer climates than ours most likely and the chances of it producing a decent crop in an average year here are slim.

Buy your seed stock from a reputable supplier who has varieties known to do well in the British climate.

It likes a sunny spot but does not need a rich soil, preferably one that has not had manure in the preceding year. Plant by dibbing holes around 20cm (8 inches) apart each way or a little less, around 8cm (3 inches) deep. Break the seed bulb up into individual cloves and drop these into the holes flat-end down. Fill the hole with soil or, better still, some fine multipurpose compost.

Larger cloves produce larger garlic bulbs; very small cloves are not worth planting if space is limited.

Garlic will not do well in a waterlogged heavy soil but you can get around this by dibbing your hole a little deeper and dropping some grit and sand into the base to ensure good drainage before dropping the clove in.

Another way to get around heavy soil is to start the garlic off in 8cm (3 inch) pots in a coldframe in November then plant out in the spring just after the leaves have appeared.

Garlic likes a long growing season and a period of cold, so sowing in November is preferred, although you can get away with an early spring sowing. Keep weed-free but otherwise do nothing unless the spring and summer are dry, in which case water.

The bulbs are harvested when the leaves turn yellow in midsummer. Use a fork to dig them up carefully.

Allow to dry off for a week or so before storing, although wet garlic, freshly harvested, is prized by many chefs and can be used immediately.

Globe Artichokes

Fig. 57. Globe artichoke.

The name artichoke is the only thing it has in common with the Jerusalem artichoke. It is considered a luxury gourmet crop, fetching high prices in the shops but requires some effort to prepare and eat as well as to grow.

It is quite an attractive plant, looking more like a decorative thistle about 1.2 metres (4 feet) tall than a vegetable crop with silvery leaves. If you are short of space for vegetables, then grow this in a flower border, where it will not be out of place.

It can be started from seed, but it is tricky and the usual method is to grow from rooted offsets (suckers), planted in early to mid spring.

In the first year, you need to ensure it is kept weed-free and watered when dry. It is quite greedy and will thank you for mulching with well rotted manure or compost, and for liquid feeding every couple of weeks.

Small heads will start to develop in the first year. Cut these off and discard to reserve strength for the next year. In the late autumn, cut off the foliage and mulch the crowns to protect them for the winter. Pile leaves or straw over the crown, using wire netting to keep it in place, and cover this with plastic sheeting to keep dry as well.

Remove the covering in early spring when the plants start to grow again, feeding after they start to produce heads in July or possibly June. Remove the main stem head first (this is called the king head), and then remove the secondary heads as they are developed. Do not allow them to develop more than six heads in this second year but thereafter you can get up to 12 heads per plant. Once cut, reduce the stem by half.

The plants will be productive for around four to six years but you can harvest rooted suckers and so grow more plants. Select from your best plants and you will improve your strain as the years go by.

To prepare in the kitchen, cut the stalk level with the base of the head, removing any damaged scales and trimming the points off the remaining scales with sharp scissors. Remove the central hairy choke, which is inedible. Boil until tender, usually around 40 minutes. You only eat the fleshy base of the scales with a dressing, leaving the point on the plate. The central fond is eaten afterwards with a spoon.

Jerusalem Artichokes

In 1621 the writer John Goodyer wrote of the Jerusalem Artichoke, ". . . in my judgement, which way soever they be drest and eaten they stir up and cause a filthie loathsome stinking winde with the bodie, thereby causing the belly to bee much pained and tormented.... more fit for swine, than men."

This may be a little harsh but the truth is that they can have quite a dramatic effect, giving them their nickname of 'farti-chokes'. The flavour is described as smoky nuts and honey and they have become quite a gourmet dish but they are not to everyone's taste. Before growing them, it is as well to try a few meals and see how everyone likes them.

They are grown in the same spot each year, for if you miss a tuber it will grow like a volunteer potato, so prepare the ground well with plenty of manure which you can top up as a mulch in winter.

Be careful where you site them, the foliage easily reaches

2 metres (6½ feet), and 2.4 metres (8 feet) is common. The stems are quite fragile and you will need to provide support with stakes and string in windy locations.

Plant individual tubers about 40–45cm (16–18 inches) apart, around 12cm (5 inches) deep, in early spring; in a few weeks the shoots will appear. If you have more than one row, allow 75cm (30 inches) between rows. When they reach about 30cm (12 inches) high, earth up a little as for potatoes.

In the autumn, the foliage starts to change colour and should be cut down to about 30cm (12 inches) above the ground as a marker. You can leave them in the ground to dig as required. They are quite a productive crop; 3kg from one plant is typical so you don't need many seed tubers.

The best variety is Fuseau, which is less knobbly and so easier for the cook. You can save your own tubers to plant in subsequent years.

Kale

Fig. 58.   Curly kale.

Kale, also called borecole, is one of the easiest and hardiest brassicas to grow. It will produce on poorer soils than the rest of the cabbage tribe will and is even tolerant of club-root to some degree. Add to that list of benefits that the curly kales are attractive in their own right and you might wonder why you don't see it on every plot. The truth is that it is an acquired taste and, in these days where any fresh vegetables can be bought in supermarkets 365 days a year, in or out of season, people are less forgiving of acquired tastes.

Having said that, the taste is much improved if you harvest young leaves rather than old and tough ones, and cook it properly.

Started in May and planted out in July, it comes in to production late in the year – November or December going right the way through March.

Kale comes in curly leaf and plain leaf varieties. The curly-leaved types are smaller and more tender than their plain-leaved cousins so are the best ones to try initially.

Kohlrabi

Fig. 59.   Kohlrabi.

Kohlrabi is another unusual vegetable in Britain, although popular in Europe. The taste is a cross between a turnip and a cabbage and the name comes from the German Khol ("cabbage") and Rabi ("turnip"). It is well worth the price of a packet of seeds to try this unusual crop.

It is a brassica but not so demanding of the soil as swedes and turnips, but it is vulnerable to club-root and cabbage root fly.

Successively sow directly in late April onwards at 1cm (½ inch) deep, in rows 30cm (12 inches) apart, thinning to 15cm (6 inches) apart for a crop from late July through to December. Harvest the ball-shaped roots when they are about

8–10cm (3½–4 inches) across and use immediately. Unlike swedes and turnips, they are not a storing crop.

Leeks

Fig. 60. Leek.

Leeks are almost a staple food in winter and, being a member of the onion family of alliums, they can provide a substitute for onions in some recipes as well. They are easy to grow and, being hardy, will stand through the winter when there is plenty of space on the plot through to spring.

The earliest crops are started under glass as early as January but more usually in March and April. They are a transplant crop and can be started in a seedbed but do best started in modules or root trainers. Sow a few seeds per module and thin to one. Starting in compost in large pots or troughs will also work but by planting time the roots will be very tangled and difficult to split.

Once the leek, looking very like a spring onion, has reached the thickness of a pencil and about 10cm (4 inches) high it can be planted out, usually in June and July.

The long white stem of the leek is caused mainly by blanching (excluding the light), so they are planted in holes. Take an old spade handle or similar and push this some 15cm (6 inches) deep into the soil, spacing between 15cm and 20cm (6 and 8 inches) apart each way. Just drop the leek into the hole and water well to settle it in.

After this, you need do little else, apart from ensuring the crop is watered in dry weather and weeding. By the end of summer, the leeks will have filled the hole and you can gently earth up around them if you wish to increase the blanched length.

Another way to increase the blanched length, without the risk of soil getting between the layers and adding an unpleasant crunch to your meal, is to collar with a toilet roll or kitchen roll cardboard inner tube. Cut the tube lengthways to enable it to be fitted and hold it on with an elastic band or similar.

If you find you have extra seedlings when it comes to planting time, these can be used in the place of spring onions in stir fries. When planted out, you can pull alternate leeks from the row, leaving those left to grow on.

Some old books advised trimming the roots and tops of the leaves before transplanting. This has been shown to be counter productive. Not all the old-fashioned methods were sound, so don't do it.

There are differences between varieties. Some mature more quickly than others and some will stand for longer through the winter so sowing two or three varieties will be best if you really like leeks and want the longest season. The seeds store for three years in the right conditions.

Leeks do best in a soil rich in humus and nutrients but are less demanding than the onion family. They do not like a waterlogged soil, which can cause rotting, but apart from rust (a fungal disease so called for the reddish rust that appears on the leaves), they are generally disease-free. You can buy rust resistant varieties now which is just as well as there is no approved chemical control for rust.

Lettuce and Salad Leaves

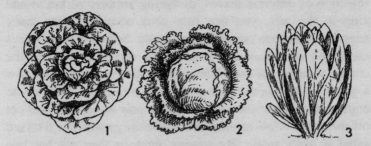

Fig. 61. Lettuce.
(1) Butterhead.
(2) Crisp heart.
(3) Cos.

Lettuce is one of those crops that you can often find bolted and going to seed on the vegetable plot so the secret is to sow little and often. The seeds are very cheap and store for three years so be ruthless: if unused and going past it, to the compost heap with them and use the space. Lettuce and salad leaves fall outside of the rotation so just fit them in where you can.

The four main types of lettuce are the cos varieties, the butterheads, loose-leafed varieties like lollo rosso and the crisphead or iceberg varieties. What you grow will depend on personal preference but the butterheads tend to be more tolerant of poor conditions.

Surprisingly, lettuce can be very hardy, enabling crops to be taken through most of the year. With a greenhouse or coldframe you can even cover the depths of winter.

Choose the appropriate variety for the time of year and sow thinly into three modules or small pots in compost. Thin to one seedling per module and plant out after a couple or three weeks, starting another batch in the pots. This successional sowing and planting will keep you in lettuce at the peak of perfection rather than the glut and famine method favoured by too many growers.

With the current fashion for mixed salads containing a selection of different leaves, including peppery rocket to add zing to the mix, you can buy seed mixtures from many suppliers based on cut and come again. Some of these mixes are based on Italian or French style salads, containing the correct varieties for each. The concept is very simple: you sow a patch, scattering the seed and leave it to grow. After six to eight weeks or so, you simply take a pair of scissors and cut off the leaves a few centimetres above the ground and a mixed salad is ready made. By sowing three or four patches two weeks apart you can ensure you always have a salad mix available, cutting round them in a circle.

Lettuce isn't too fussy about the soil, although it prefers a good level of humus in the soil and a sunny spot. Especially at the cold ends of the season, it will not thank you for a wet soil.

There are a number of troubles that can beset the lettuce. The most common, as usual, is the slug, and aphids can be a problem too (just wash them off), but usually lettuces are trouble free. Bolting, where the heart grows upwards, and brown edges to the leaves are caused by an irregular water supply or exceptionally hot weather.

If they do not seem to do well after planting, try another area of the plot for the next planting which is the best answer for most problems.

Onions

Fig. 62.　Onion – with onion sets on the left.

The onion is a kitchen staple that home growing transforms. You can choose a variety that suits your taste from mild to so strong they can be considered tear gas when cut.

Onions are either grown from seeds or sets, which are effectively small bulbs.

Sets are easier for beginners, although starting from seed isn't really difficult. The sets have a head start so they get off quickly, are more disease resistant, avoid the onion fly, crop better in poorer soils and will usually provide a crop even if they go in later than they should.

Seeds, however, are cheaper to buy and are available in far more varieties. They are also less prone to bolting and seem to store better as well.

You can get overwintering onions, often called Japanese onions, and these do seem to do better from sets than seed. They do not store well but do fill the gap until the main crop arrives a month later. These are planted from mid-September to early November to provide a crop for June.

Whether you grow seeds or sets, the soil needs to be in good heart and not too soggy because a heavy wet soil will encourage fungal rots in the crop. Sets are a little more tolerant of poor nutrient levels but add a general purpose fertilizer a week before you plant for best results.

Sets are planted fat-end down, so that the tip is just above soil level, in March and April. You can plant 15cm (6 inches) apart each way or spaced at 10cm (4 inches) in rows 20–30cm (8–12 inches) apart. Closer spacing produces smaller bulbs but there is no point going over 15cm (6 inches) apart unless you are trying to grow giants. Incidentally, large sets are more prone to bolting so do not discard small sets in the pack in favour of them.

Scrape a small hole or a drill to plant in, then backfill the soil. Just pushing the sets into the soil, especially a heavier soil, can damage the root plate and kill the set.

The biggest problem with sets are birds who like to pull them out of the soil. Netting or even cloching until established is advisable.

Onions from seed should be started earlier, since they don't have the head start of a set. Usually early March is about right. You can sow directly but much better results will come from starting off under glass in modules, 15 to a seed tray, at a temperature between 10–15° Celsius.

Once germinated, do not let the temperature rise above 15° Celsius or the onions will get confused about what time of year it is and bolt later after they're planted out. Move out of the greenhouse into a cold frame and harden off before planting out, spaced as for the sets. The beauty of this method is that the onions can be held if the weather is bad until you are ready to plant.

With both set planted and seed sown, there is little to do apart from keep weed-free and water in dry weather until harvest time. You can pull at any point for immediate use but, for onions to store, wait until the foliage is starting to bend over of its own accord. You will read in old books about bending the foliage over – do not do it because it causes damage to the neck, creating problems in storage.

Just gently lever under the bulbs with a fork and then dry them out for storage. The ideal is to place them on some sort of rack outdoors where air can flow all around them for a couple of weeks. If the weather is really wet, you need to provide some sort of cover; the odd shower will not cause any harm though. Be careful about drying onions in a greenhouse. If it gets really hot, then you end up starting to cook them and they won't store.

Once they have dried out, string them up and hang in a cool, dark place. Occasionally check the base of the bulbs for rot starting and remove those bulbs to prevent it spreading.

Onions are susceptible to rust, smut mildew and white tip, where the leaves go white from the tip down the stem. There is no chemical treatment available to the gardener but a spray with seaweed fertilizer may help prevent its spread. White rot, where a white fungus grows on the base of the bulb, killing the plant, is serious and there is no treatment. Avoid growing on the same spot for eight years or grow in large containers or raised beds with bought-in compost. It is the club-root of onions, being easily spread and difficult to cope with.

The main pest is the onion fly where small maggots, 5–10mm long eat the base of the bulb. Grow from sets if this is a constant problem or try keeping under fleece or cloche until well established.

Bolting, where the plant sends up a flower shoot, is a fairly common problem. Cut off this flower stem when seen and use those onions first as they will not store well.

Parsnips

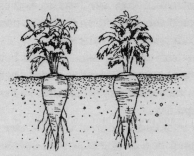

Fig. 63.   Parsnip.

The parsnip is another underrated crop, which is a shame as it is delicious if cooked properly, as well as a good source of calcium in the diet.

Like other root crops they like a friable soil, rich in humus but not manured the previous year. If you have a heavy soil, select a suitable shorter rooted variety or grow in raised beds filled with finer soil and compost.

You will often be told to sow in February and that parsnips have a poor germination rate. Since in February the soil is often cold and wet, this should be no surprise. Sowing in March or April will produce a perfectly good crop and germination rates miraculously improve. Since the flavour of parsnips is improved by a few good frosts, there is little benefit to an early crop.

Parsnip seed does not store. Use when you open the packet and discard any left over. Sow thinly in rows 30cm (12 inches) apart, 1–2cm (¾ inch) deep and thin to around 15cm (6 inches) apart. Germination can be spotty but you can try station sowing three seeds, each 15cm (6 inches), and then thin to one seedling. Whichever way you choose, it is important not to overcrowd the plants; the foliage grows quite large, and overcrowding results in very small parsnips.

Apart from weeding and watering in a dry summer, there is nothing else to do until after the first few frosts when you can lift the crop. Parsnips can be left in the ground over winter but if the ground is frozen they are hard to harvest so mulching with straw to keep the ground workable is useful. Otherwise store as other root crops in a dark shed.

Do not leave them in the ground beyond February because they will start to re-grow, using the stored energy in the root. In mild winters, they can start this earlier so harvesting is best completed in January.

They can be attacked by carrot root fly (see page 112) but this is not as much of a problem as with carrots. Slugs can be a bit of a pest as well, causing minor damage to the crown (top of the root).

One major problem is canker, causing a blackened area towards the crown and the root to rot. There are various causes – lack of lime, irregular water supply and manure in the soil seem to spark the problem off. The best answer is to grow resistant varieties which are common and you may never see the problem.

Peas

Fig. 64. Peas, showing them properly supported on wires.

The humble pea is one of our oldest vegetables, having been eaten for at least five thousand years and is one of our most popular vegetables today. Peas are good for you as well, being a good source of riboflavin, vitamin B6, magnesium, phosphorus and potassium, and a very good source of dietary fibre, vitamin A, vitamin C, vitamin K, thiamine, iron and manganese. Raw peas, by the way, contain four times as much vitamin C than cooked peas so adding them raw to a salad is a great way to eat healthily.

The sweetness of the pea comes from natural sugars and these sugars convert to starch when picked, so the sweetest peas are the freshest. They are edible raw. Try them straight from the pod on the plot and you will be amazed just how sweet they are.

The popularity of the pea means that there are a large number of varieties which fall into these groups.

The **wrinkled varieties**, also known as marrowfat peas, which, when dried, are wrinkled. They tend not to be hardy but are more popular than other types as they produce heavier crops.

These are further sub-divided by the height they grow (dwarf varieties at 45–60cm/18–24 inches and tall varieties at up to 2 metres/6½ feet) and how quickly they develop.

The first earlies take around 11 weeks to start cropping, second earlies 13–14 weeks and the maincrop 15–16 weeks.

The **round varieties**, where when dried the pea is smooth, are more hardy and dwarf types. They are all first earlies and usually sown as a first crop when frost still threatens, although they can be sown at the end of the year to provide a last quick crop before the cold weather properly sets in. You can sow some round varieties in October/November with a view to a very early crop the following year but, as with winter-sown broad beans, failure rates are high and early-spring-sown beans under cloche will often catch up anyway.

Mangetout peas – also called eat all, Chinese peas, snap peas or sugar peas just to confuse you – are bred so that the whole pod is eaten. They should be picked young before the peas swell.

Petits Pois are specially-bred small and very sweet peas, not just ordinary peas cropped small. They are a gourmet delight and worth growing, despite not being the most productive.

Peas are legumes and produce their own nitrogen, so a manure rich soil is not needed but they do like a lot of humus in the soil and a pH approaching neutral. They do not like being waterlogged, which a good level of humus will prevent.

For the earliest crop, cloche a week before sowing direct in late February to early March. One method of starting an early crop is to fill a length of roof guttering with compost and sow into that in a greenhouse. When the shoots appear, draw a trench outside and very carefully slide the content of the gutter into the trench. However, this method is unlikely to be any more successful than sowing under cloche and transferring to the soil is a tricky business.

Normally peas are sown in a trench about 15cm (6 inches) wide and 3–5cm (about 2 inches) deep. The peas are dropped into the trench about 8cm (3 inches) apart in two staggered rows. A second 'double row' can be sown, spaced the expected height of the crop from the first.

Another method is to block sow equidistant 8cm (3 inches) apart. When sown this way, some varieties will be self-supporting and not need staking.

With the dwarf varieties in rows, the usual method is to use pea sticks. These are usually the twigs left from pruning bushes, etc., and are inserted into the trench at sowing time to provide a structure for the peas to climb and keep their pods off the soil.

With tall varieties, insert firm stakes at 90cm (36 inches) or less intervals and attach pea netting right by the row. Once a mass of foliage has climbed this net, it acts as a sail, catching the wind, so it is important for it to be soundly constructed.

Feeding is not strictly required if the soil is in good heart but, if you have spare liquid comfrey fertilizer available, a feed when the pods begin to form is beneficial.

Peas develop upwards so harvest from the bottom. Leaving mature pods on the plant will stop new pods from forming, as with runner beans, so little and often. A glut of peas is easily frozen, the sooner after picking the better. You can home-dry peas to store them; indeed they were always eaten as dried peas in stews, etc., until the seventeenth century in Britain when somebody had the bright idea of trying them fresh.

Peas are not a troublesome crop but they are attractive to birds and mice when sown. Sowing under cloche will keep the birds off but mice can still be troublesome. Laying spiky gorse clippings or holly leaves over the peas when sown, before drawing the soil over, is one suggested preventative.

The main trouble with the crop is the pea moth that lays its eggs at flowering time, producing nasty little maggots in the peas. If it is a major problem in your area, you can use fleece to keep it off. It is active mid-May to mid-June so early and late sowings will miss the pest.

It is easy to spot and, if processing a large number of peas to freeze, dropping them into cold water before blanching will reveal the maggots in the floaters.

Potatoes

Fig. 65.   Potatoes, almost ready to harvest.

A lot of new vegetable growers seem to find potatoes awfully complex yet they are a simple vegetable to grow successfully and once you have tasted your own potatoes you will know why they are worth growing. The difference between home-grown potatoes and supermarket potatoes is unbelievable.

Unlike most vegetables, potatoes prefer the soil slightly acid so you want to put them at the far end of lime in your crop rotation. They are, however, greedy feeders so a goodly amount of manure or compost worked into the soil will help to feed them, as well as improving the texture of the soil.

The big benefit of growing potatoes must be the taste, and you have a choice of over four hundred varieties to choose from – a few hundred more than you will ever find in the shops. So you need to decide what you want to grow. First of all, ask other growers in your area what they do well with and like. Different varieties will grow better in some areas than others. Next read the description from your supplier. Usually there is some guidance on what the potato is like, if it is a salad type or a good chipper, etc.

You can often buy small packs of 10 seed potatoes so you can try different types and find what you like.

Do not just try and plant potatoes from the supermarket. More often than not you will be wasting your time if they have been treated to prevent sprouting and risking disease – not to mention you will be missing an opportunity to taste something really special for your efforts.

Good quality seed potatoes will be marked as 'certified' meaning the grower is approved and the stock is disease-free. They should be about the size of a hen's egg, free from damage and not shrivelled. Neither should they be sprouting when you purchase them.

There is some evidence that larger seed potatoes produce better crops and certainly very small seed potatoes will fail to crop well.

The terms First Early, Second Early and Maincrop Potatoes often sound mysterious but they're not really. All the terms refer to is the time it takes from planting to getting a crop. First earlies are usually ready in around ten weeks, second earlies in around 13 weeks and maincrop after about 20 weeks.

Maincrop types tend to store better but they are at more risk of getting blight than the faster types, which are usually harvested before the blight periods begin.

Chitting Potatoes

There is no mystery to this process. All it means is that when you get your seed potatoes you put them in a cool but frost-free place where they get some light but not direct sunlight. A north-facing window is ideal in a frost-free shed.

The potatoes will then grow short stubby shoots, which will get them off to a fast start when planted out. Some people suggest rubbing off all but three shoots to help get larger potatoes with the maincrops.

Frost is a big enemy so you need to keep an eye on the weather. Usually mid-March is about the right time to plant your earlies and you plant the maincrop a few weeks later. If after planting, the leaves (also called haulm) start to show through and frost threatens, you need to protect the plants. You can do this by pulling earth over the haulm from the side or covering with fleece.

To plant, you can just make a hole with a trowel and pop the seed potato in or you can draw a trench (take a draw hoe and scrape a trench) and place the potatoes in it.

You want it to be about 10cm (4 inches) deep. You then pull the soil from the sides to cover the potatoes.

If you have a comfrey patch, try and get a cut of comfrey leaves, allow to wilt for a day and just place them on the bottom of your trench. Comfrey will quickly rot down to provide fertilizer and it is almost perfect for potatoes and tomatoes.

Your first and second early potatoes should be planted about 30cm (12 inches) apart, in rows about 60cm (24 inches) apart. The maincrop, being the heaviest cropper, need a bit more space so plant them about 40cm (16 inches) apart, in rows 75cm (30 inches) apart.

As the plants grow, you need to draw the earth from the sides of your rows over the plants. The potato tubers (that's what we call the actual potato you eat) tend to grow towards the surface and if light gets to them they will go green. You do not want to eat green potatoes as they may give you upset stomach, so 'earthing up', as this is called, will cover these tubers and increase your crop.

It won't hurt the plants or slow down the growth when you cover some of the leaves by earthing up.

I mentioned they are greedy feeders and an additional dose of fertilizer after a month or so when the plants are established will really help. You can use specifically formulated potato fertilizer or a general organic fertilizer such as fish, blood and bone. Good results can be had from using a liquid comfrey feed because the liquid is immediately available.

In dry weather, keep them well watered. They produce a lot of crop and need their water. If the water supply is irregular, the yield will be reduced and the potatoes can be cracked from uneven growth.

Harvesting Potatoes

Your first earlies are your new potatoes. When they are nearly ready you can sacrifice a plant to get a delicious meal. Just take a plant at a time as the rest will be continuing to grow and swell up.

Approach from the side with a fork and lift, trying to avoid spearing your crop. However, you always manage to fork a few – it's the nature of the beast, I'm afraid.

The rest of the crop can be dug up in whole rows when they are mature. Try and pick a dry sunny day and leave them on the surface for a few hours to harden the skin. This will help them store better.

Do try even to get tiny potatoes out or next year they'll be growing and acting as a reservoir for pests and disease.

Storing Potatoes

The best way to store your potatoes is in hessian sacks that you can buy from many of the seed suppliers. You need to exclude light, or the potato will turn green, but allow them to breathe and for moisture to evaporate. Check them carefully and use any damaged ones first or rot will spread through the whole sack. It is well worth emptying your sacks after a month or so to make sure none is rotting. Throw a few slug pellets into the sacks. They can't hurt wildlife but will attract and kill any slugs that have got in without you noticing.

Do not allow your potatoes to freeze; the ideal storage temperature is around 5° Celsius but freezing will cause them to taste strange and may start them rotting. To cure this taste, bring them into the house and store at 15–18° Celsius for a week before using.

Potato Pests and Troubles

Your worst enemy is undoubtedly the slug. So, do whatever you normally do for slugs but double it. Nematodes are very effective and are organically approved as a slug control.

Blight is the next worst problem (see potato blight on page

117). There are other problems but slugs and blight are the ones that hit most of us and usually potatoes are pretty easy to get a decent crop.

Pumpkins and Squashes

Pumpkins and squashes (along with marrows and courgettes) are cucurbits and, although we give them different names, they actually blend into each other. The pumpkins come in various sizes from gigantic to the size of a football, and squashes from ball-shaped to all sorts of strange-looking fruits.

Their requirements are similar: plenty of food, water and some good weather. Started in pots in April or directly sown and planted out in May under cloche, they produce the fruit for summer and autumn. Sow the flat seed on its side (thin side vertical to stop water sitting on the seed) to prevent rotting off.

If you wish to grow a really large pumpkin, which can be so large you may need mechanical assistance to move it, you can. Dig a hole around 60cm (24 inches) in all dimensions and fill with a mixture of compost and well rotted manure. Leave the top slightly mounded and add some general purpose fertilizer a week or two before planting into it.

Once one small fruit has started to form, pinch off any other fruits as they form and commence weekly feeding with liquid tomato fertilizer. Put a pallet, a strong one in good condition, under the pumpkin. This will ensure air gets under it and stops it from rotting on the ground.

There are all sorts of magic mixtures used by real giant pumpkin enthusiasts but this strategy will produce a pumpkin guaranteed to impress. The current favourite giant variety is Atlantic Giant but Hundredweight produces similar results.

For normal edible pumpkins and squashes (the giants are technically edible) a smaller planting hole, just 30cm (12 inches) cubed will be sufficient. Trailing varieties need room, so plant around 1.2 metres (4 feet) apart. You can maximize the use of space by guiding the leaves in a spiral. Feeding is still needed for the best crop but once a fortnight will be enough.

Keep the number of fruits down to a reasonable number for the variety. For pumpkins this is usually two or four per plant and around six for a squash. Inserting a sheet of glass or some other barrier between fruit and soil will prevent rotting where they touch the soil.

The standard butternut squash is a consistent, reliable cropper and one of the best in terms of flavour, and the vegetable spaghetti varieties are popular with cooks as well. Summer custard squashes are very similar to courgettes in flavour although the shape, scallop-edged discs, is very different.

The bush varieties of summer squash can be extremely prolific; one plant per variety is sufficient per household and often for a few friends as well.

When the fruits of the winter storing varieties are mature, remove from the plant, cutting the stalk a few centimetres from the fruit. Place somewhere sheltered and sunny to allow the skin to harden off and then store in a cool dark place. A slatted shelf is best, allowing air flow all round, or string up in a net bag or even in an old pair of tights. Storage times vary but pumpkins will keep until Christmas and butternut squash can last into February or even longer.

The biggest pest to worry about is the slug, so keep your defences up. Mice and rats can be a problem as well, nibbling the fruit, but this rarely happens. Generally, it is a very trouble-free crop.

Radish

Fig. 66.   A row of radishes (small globe type).

The normal salad radish is one of the fastest and easiest crops to grow, which makes it ideal for getting children interested and enthused in gardening. They can be ready in as little as 18 days from sowing.

Although they are a brassica and theoretically susceptible to club-root, in practice they develop too quickly to be bothered. Two pests do bother them, slugs nibbling the root and flea beetles, both of which are covered in pests.

The radish is, because of its speed, very much a 'fit-in crop'. Where there is a small space, sow a pinch of seed thinly – about 3cm (just over an inch) apart is ideal – and rake in or cover with a centimetre of soil. As long as there is sufficient water, they should develop.

Once grown, they very quickly go woody and then to seed, so sow weekly in the salad season to ensure a continuous supply. Don't bother if they go over, the seed is cheap so compost and harvest the ones sown the week after. In hot summers, they benefit from some shade and can be grown in the shadow of other crops.

The most well known variety is French Breakfast, which is white at the tip and red at the crown, but there are many other salad varieties available which can be grown.

Although we think of radish as a summer salad crop there are winter varieties, Japanese types or mooli radishes. These grow much larger, with roots up to 30cm (12 inches) long. Since they are in the ground much longer, the soil needs more preparation as for other root crops and club-root becomes a consideration.

Rhubarb

No allotment or vegetable plot is complete without a rhubarb patch, although it is used as a fruit.

There are a few myths about rhubarb that need dispelling. The leaves are poisonous to eat, containing oxalic acid, but are perfectly safe to compost. The leaves can be shredded and boiled in water for half an hour (500g to 1 litre of water) to make an insecticidal spray for aphids and spider mites but, unfortunately, it is not true that dropping a piece of rhubarb into the planting hole will prevent club-root from affecting brassicas.

Rhubarb will be in the same place for many years (ten is not uncommon) so prepare a bed with a good depth of topsoil, at least 50cm (20 inches), with plenty of organic matter. It needs plenty of nitrogen to fuel the leaf growth so adding rotted manure will be helpful.

You can start rhubarb from seed but it takes longer to produce fruit and often doesn't result in plants true to type so it is better to start from plants, which are known as 'crowns'.

You can make crowns yourself by digging up a plant over five years old and just split it into three with a spade vertically.

You plant the crowns just a couple of centimetres under the surface, about a metre apart (40 inches) each way, any time between late October and February but rhubarb is best planted in March. After that, there is little care needed apart from weeding and feeding. When the leaves die down in late autumn, mulch them with compost or preferably rotted manure and give a handful of general purpose fertilizer like fish, blood and bone per plant in February just as they start growing again.

In the first year after planting do not harvest any sticks, allow the plants to establish well and in the second year only take a few sticks per plant. After that, you can remove all but a few sticks each year.

Forcing rhubarb produces the sweetest crop and so tender that you do not need to peel before cooking. Just place a large container over a plant, like a black plastic dustbin, as soon as it commences growing. The extra warmth will promote growth and after about four weeks a crop of pale sweet sticks can be taken.

Leave the plants to recover for at least a year, or better still two years, before cropping again. Forcing the same plant year after year will exhaust and kill it.

Different varieties of rhubarb will crop best at different times so with a range of varieties you can have a crop right from April through to August.

Timperley Early is generally considered best for an early crop and for forcing, with Victoria providing a late crop. Glaskin's Perpetual is a popular variety as you can actually take some sticks in the first year.

Generally rhubarb is trouble-free but you can get crown rot and honey fungus in them. Both are incurable: dig up and burn the plants, then plant new stock as far away from them on the plot as possible.

Runner Beans

Fig. 67.   Runner beans arranged on sticks.

If any crop sums up vegetable growing it is the runner bean. No allotment site is without its rows of runner beans and it is one crop that seems subject to waste since it is very productive and the family often tires well before the plant finishes.

Runner beans were first grown for their decorative flowers and only later were the beans discovered to be edible. Painted Lady is probably the most decorative variety and will form an attractive backdrop to a flower border. They can be success-fully grown up a wigwam in a large pot, 50cm (20 inches) or more, so long as sufficient water is given with a monthly feed of tomato fertilizer.

Being so productive, the plant is a little demanding, liking a humus-rich soil with, like the broad bean, additional potash. To produce the crop, it also requires plenty of water and this was the reason for the traditional bean trench.

Started in winter, the bean trench was about 20–30cm (8–12 inches) deep and a spade blade in width. It was lined with sheets of newspaper and the contents of the kitchen wastebin were added, covering with soil to stop vermin. By May this was reduced well and would ensure water was held available for the season. Often permanent supports were erected with metal poles to avoid the chore of erecting bamboo canes each year but this practice encouraged the build-up of fungal disease and they should be rotated as many gardeners have discovered to their cost.

The traditional method was a row of sticks or bamboo canes at 25cm (10 inch) spacing, in a double row 30–40cm (12–16 inches) apart, angled to meet at the top with a horizontal support.

An easier method than constructing the traditional row of canes is to insert 2.4m (8 feet) bamboo poles at 25cm (10 inch) spacing in a circle tied at the top to form a wigwam. You can even get a plastic circle to hold the canes which is easier than tying at the top.

Beans can be trained up strings in a maypole arrangement as well, although constructing this so the strings are held taut to the ground can be tricky.

Runner beans are not hardy – a late frost will destroy your plants – so the favoured method is to start off in pots under glass in early May to plant out when the risk of frost is past in June. You can sow direct, at a depth of 5cm (2 inches), by the base of the poles. If a late frost does arrive, protect with fleece or even newspapers overnight. In the worst case of losing the first sowing, don't despair because a late sowing in June will still produce a respectable crop.

When the plants reach the top of the poles, pinch out the

growing tip to encourage bushier growth. Once the pods start to form, you can harvest them young and tender or leave to grow longer. If you want large beans for eating, then look for varieties described as 'stringless'. Some varieties such as Enorma tend to produce larger pods.

If you find you have more crop of beans than you want, leave the pods to swell and you can harvest the beans which are good in stews. Leaving them longer when the pods will dry off will produce free seed for you for next year.

Dwarf varieties of runner bean like Hestia can be used to provide a very early crop by growing in a 20cm (8 inch) pot in the frost-free greenhouse; starting them off in mid-March will give you a few out-of-season meals before the main crops come in late July to run through October.

Runner beans will store well frozen but they do taste that bit better fresh.

Salsify and Scorzonera

Fig. 68. Salsify.

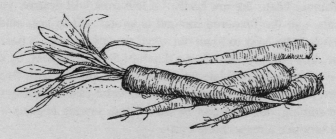

Fig. 69. Scorzonera.

These are root crops, very rarely seen in the shops because they are not commonly known and so not popular yet their flavour is considered far superior to parsnips, which they resemble although with a thinner root. Salsify is often referred to as the vegetable oyster due to its subtle flavour. Scorzonera is similar in flavour but has a black-skinned root.

They require a good depth of light soil and are well suited to growing in raised deep beds and large containers. Like other root crops, do not manure the year before as that will cause the plants to fork (or split). They do benefit from the addition of a general purpose fertilizer the week before sowing.

Sow three seeds per position direct in late April, early May at 15cm (6 inch) spacing, 1.5cm (¾ inch) deep, thinning out to one plant per station. Weed carefully because the crown is easily damaged; hand-weeding rather than hoeing is best.

They are trouble-free, just water in dry weather. Harvest can begin mid-October and they can stay in the ground through to February or even March, although harvesting in frozen ground will be very difficult as the 30cm (12 inch) long roots are quite fragile.

Harvesting in November will be easier. Store as for parsnips and carrots but they do tend to dry out and wrinkle in store. Preparation is more difficult than the humble parsnip, scalding will make the skin easier to scrape off and then steam or boil until tender. Boiling and then peeling is recommended by some chefs. The difficulties in preparation are repaid with the taste.

Shallots

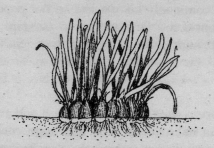

Fig. 70. Shallot, shown both above and below ground.

Prized by chefs for their mild flavour, shallots have another big advantage over onions in that they store for longer – nine months is common and a year if kept in good conditions so covering any gap when the stored onions have gone over.

You can get shallot seed but they are normally grown from sets. Prepare the soil as for onions and plant about 15–20cm (6–8 inches) each way between plants. They can be planted to overwinter or planted in very early spring to be ready for mid-summer.

They are subject to the same problems as onions, with a tendency to bolt in hot summers but generally easy enough to grow. They are harvested as a clump with the individual bulbs in a ring. There is no need to split them apart until you come to use them.

Spinach

Fig. 71. Spinach.

Despite the claims of Popeye, spinach actually has no more vitamins than many other vegetables. True spinach is not the easiest of crops to grow either, especially when compared to the beet leaf perpetual spinach, but the taste is a little superior.

The two main types are summer and winter spinach. Summer spinach has a habit of bolting in warm sunny weather but enjoys some shade, so try growing a row in the shadow of a tall crop of peas or sweetcorn.

Both types need a good rich soil, with plenty of available nitrogen to power the leaf growth, and plenty of water as well. Successionally sow summer spinach in April and May, winter spinach in August and September. Both are thinly sown about 2–3cm (1 inch) deep, in rows 30cm (12 inches) apart, thinning to 10cm (4 inches) apart as soon as they show. When they have developed a little, remove every other plant for use in the kitchen.

Pick young leaves from the outside of the plant as required. With summer spinach you can take up to half the leaves in one go but be more gentle with winter spinach. Use immediately. A seemingly large number of leaves will go down in the pan to quite a small amount.

Spinach is very much a 'love it or hate it' vegetable. If you love it, it is worth persevering and growing the true spinach.

Spring Onions

Spring onions tend to be treated as an afterthought by most gardening books yet they are a popular crop and very useful. Salad onions, also properly called scallions, are easily grown and can substitute for bulb onions if stocks are low.

They like a rich well drained soil but, being a useful crop to fill into gaps in the summer, they tend to get what they are given. It's a good idea to give some general purpose fertilizer a week before and rake the soil into a fine tilth before sowing them.

Conventionally they are grown in rows 15cm (6 inches) apart but can more easily just be thinly scattered in a patch and either raked in or covered with 1.5cm (¾ inch) of fine soil.

Successionally sow each week or two from early March for a continuous supply. Late sowings in August, September and a fine October will provide an early spring crop. Use a winter hardy variety. White Lisbon is the best known variety but look for White Lisbon Winter Hardy for the overwinter sowing.

A red spring onion is available as well: North Holland Blood Red. This has the benefit that you can sow a patch, removing as required and any left will just bulb up.

Spring onions do not need a great depth of soil and a winter crop can be grown in the greenhouse in a pot filled with compost.

There are few problems with spring onions as long as the soil can provide enough nutrition.

Strawberries

Strawberries, although a fruit, are often found on the vegetable plot. They are not normally considered in crop rotations as the plants have a limited lifespan and, therefore, each generation can move around a plot with the rotation. Alternatively, a number of separate strawberry beds can be maintained, allowing for a rest between years.

Strawberries do well in strawberry barrels where the plants make use of the compost in the barrel being planted into the sides. These also maximize production for the area in this way.

There are two main types of strawberries: the normal that crop over a short period, usually around three weeks, and the perpetual that produce flushes of fruit over the whole season.

Some varieties will crop early and others late, some are ideal for eating fresh and some for jam, so having a number of varieties is required to cover all your needs.

They like their soil slightly acid and are not a very hungry crop although they will benefit from $500g/m^2$ of bonemeal prior to planting.

They are usually started from plants rather than seed,

planting out in March or April. Normally planted with 20cm–25cm (8–10 inches) between plants, you need to be careful how you plant. They need to have the growing point just above the surface and the roots shallowly spread just under the soil. Make a shallow wide hole then mound up the soil into an inverted 'V' mound in the centre just below soil level. Place the plant on the mound and spread the roots down the sides.

Strawberries propagate naturally from runners. These are shoots that form small plants along their length. In the first year after planting, remove all runners as soon as you notice them. From your second and third year plants you can allow the odd runner to develop and, using a piece of wire (coathanger wire is ideal), bent into a 'V', clip the plantlet on the runner down into a small pot of compost. Cut the runner before the next plantlet. By the end of the season you have a new plant for free!

By the end of three years, the plants are past their best and should be dug out and replaced, preferably somewhere else on the plot or in fresh compost with your new plants.

The biggest problems with strawberries are mould, rot and slugs. To stop mould and rot keep the fruits off the ground by mulching under with straw or planting through weed-suppressant fabric.

At the end of the season the plants die back and this is time to clean them up. A trim, just above ground level, with shears will remove foliage, and any pests hiding within will be moved or exposed to the birds. Often gardeners in the old days would set fire to the straw, burning off the dead foliage and pests in one operation.

Strawberry plants are hardy, but their fruits are not. The season can be extended at both ends by using cloches. Commercially strawberries are grown in polytunnels in the UK to provide the longest growing season.

Swedes

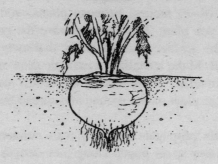

Fig. 72.   Swede.

The swede is very similar to the turnip, the name being a contraction of 'Swedish turnip' and, although it is nothing like a cabbage, it is a member of the brassica family and club-root will be a problem if you have this on your plot. Cabbage root fly can also be a problem but unlike the cabbages, where a protective circle can be placed around the stem, this is not feasible with swedes, although covering with fleece can offer some protection. The only other real problem is the flea beetle.

Sow thinly 1cm (½ inch) deep, in rows 40cm (16 inches) apart, in May and June, thinning out in stages until the plants are 20/25cm (8/10 inches) apart. Keep watered in dry periods to avoid woody texture and split skins, and start harvesting in November. Leave in the ground, slowly growing, lifting as required through to March.

You can harvest and store as for other root crops if you prefer but swedes are at their best within a week of being picked.

Although often used in soups and stews, swedes also work well as a mashed vegetable. Cut into cubes and boil for 30 minutes, drain and mash with butter, cream and pepper. You can also add a little powdered ginger or nutmeg to add some zing. They can be a little sloppy, so try mixing fifty/fifty with mashed potatoes.

Sweetcorn

Fig. 73. Sweetcorn.

Sweetcorn used to be a very difficult crop outside of the south of the country as it needed a long, warm growing season to succeed but the development of new varieties changed all that. The 'super sweet' F1 varieties are exceptionally tasty but never inter-mix varieties as they cross-pollinate, making the results unpredictable. If you do grow two varieties, separate them by at least 8 metres (nearly 27 feet) to avoid this.

The cliché is that you should put a pan of water to boil, harvest your cob and run, not walk, to the pan to enjoy the best flavour, since the moment it is removed from the plant the sugars begin to turn to starch.

In reality, the sweetcorn will keep reasonably well for a week or so in the salad drawer of the fridge and a glut can be frozen either on or off the cob. As well as boiling, sweetcorn is a great vegetable to barbecue – leave the leaves on to protect the corn, as it cooks in its own steam.

It still requires a long season but the biggest reasons for failure to get a good crop are overcrowding and under-feeding. It produces a mass of tall foliage and needs a lot of nitrogen to power that growth, along with space for it. Never crowd sweetcorn: allow at least 45cm (18 inches) each way because it is planted in blocks rather than rows to encourage pollination. Poor pollination results in patchy development of the corn kernels.

Sow towards the end of April or in early May under cover.

With sweetcorn, chitting the seed is often worthwhile. Take a shallow container and lay a sheet of damp kitchen paper in the base, place the seeds on the paper and cover with another sheet of damp paper. Put the lid on the container and place in a warm (around 20° Celsius) dark place. An airing cupboard is ideal. After three days check carefully to see if any have sprouted, then check daily after that. Generally, they will all sprout within a day or two of each other.

As soon as you see them start, you must plant around 3cm (1 inch) deep in an 8cm (3 inch) pot or into root trainers in multi-purpose compost. Root trainers are deep modules that open up to enable easy planting and are excellent for plants that have long roots that do not like disturbance.

You can also save toilet roll inner tubes and fill these with compost as a pot. The tube is planted out and rots away in the soil. Although some consider this method fine, the cardboard inner tubes tend to dry out easily so you need to check daily; spraying the tubes with water helps to prevent this. Re-usable pots are an easier option.

The pots need not be kept quite as warm as the seeds but you want them over 10° Celsius. Watch out for cold night temperatures and cover with fleece in cold weather. Once the pots have been started, cloche or cover the soil with fleece where you intend to plant to pre-warm the soil. When the plants are approaching 10cm (4 inches) high, the roots will be pushing at the other end and it is time to plant out.

Make a hole 5cm (2 inches) deeper than your pot and plant into that, filling to the same level so the plant is in a little depression in the soil. Unless your soil is very rich, having been manured the preceding winter, sprinkle a little dried blood or sulphate of ammonia around each plant to provide a nitrogen boost and to get them growing away quickly. Cover with the cloche and leave this on until the plants are pushing them off of their own accord.

When the plants reach 60cm (24 inches) or so high, draw

soil up to the stem, filling in the depression and a little above. This will encourage additional root grow to power the plant.

Apart from hoeing once or twice, there is nothing else to do until June when a liquid feed will help boost the cob production. Comfrey feed is ideal, otherwise a general purpose liquid fertilizer is fine.

When the tassels that hang from the cobs turn brown they are ready to harvest.

This method is quite fussy but it never fails to produce a good crop with a high germination rate from an expensive seed. Alternatively, you can directly sow in mid-May. Drop two seeds in a hole about 3cm (just over 1 inch) deep and remove the weaker plant if both develop. Covering with a cloche is still desirable but you can try using clear plastic 2-litre bottles, with the base cut off, over each plant as a mini-cloche.

If at any time the leaves look yellowish or the plants do not seem to be growing quickly, try a high nitrogen liquid feed. The effect is usually a fast recovery.

Tomato

The tomato is one of the most popular crops for the home grower. The huge range of seeds available means that not only can you grow varieties that are not available in the shops, because they may taste wonderful but not travel or store well, but you can also grow the specific varieties that you personally like. The flavour of a tomato straight from the vine, sun warm rather than fridge cool, is sublime.

Yet tomatoes have an undeserved reputation as a hard crop to grow since the basic rules of cultivation are ignored too often by gardeners. Many of the problems discussed in detail in books and magazines are comparatively rare so long as enough attention is paid to detail.

With literally hundreds of varieties to choose from, many growers insist on the same type each year. Often these are ones developed for the commercial grower and, whilst they may produce a consistent crop of reasonable quality, taking a risk with a couple of unknown, new varieties each year can be incredibly rewarding.

Tomatoes can be grown outdoors in Britain and, with the current warmer summers, this is less risky than in years past. However, generally they do best in the greenhouse. Some varieties are bred more for outdoors and others more for the greenhouse, so reading the seed catalogue carefully before choosing is a must. Tomatoes come in different sizes from cherries right up to large 500g (1 lb) marmande types. Colours range from yellow to reds so dark that they're almost black – and there is even a green-and-yellow-striped variety! Flavours range from stingingly tart to so sweet you can convince vegetable-hating children that they are sweets.

Apart from the size and colour, tomatoes come in three main types. The first and most common is the tall **indeterminate or cordon** types. With these, the side shoots will grow out, sub-dividing and producing a giant bush if not stopped by pinching out.

The second is the **bush or determinate** type of tomato where the side branches develop naturally, forming a bush that stops itself eventually. No pinching out of the side shoots is required.

Dwarf varieties are very small bush types, often grown in hanging baskets or small containers.

For the greenhouse it is best to stick with cordon types; the bush types take up too much space. Tomatoes will do well in a polytunnel but the higher light level in a greenhouse will bring the crop on faster and help ripening.

All tomatoes are started off in heat (either a propagator or warm window sill will be fine), sowing the seeds in a small shallow pot, then moving along into an 8cm (3 inch) pot when large enough to handle. Varieties for the greenhouse can be started earlier than varieties for outdoor, usually in early March.

They will be ready for planting on into their final home by the beginning of May. If May is cold, some night heating at least will be helpful as they do not grow well below 10° Celsius.

The eventual crop will depend on how well the plant is developed and its ability to convert nutrients into fruit. This in turn will depend on the roots. The better the root development, the better the plant.

When you plant out, if you look closely at the base of the stem you will notice thin hairs growing there; these 'hairs' will turn into roots if they are in the soil so plant deeply and you produce more roots to boost growth quickly.

Planting in the greenhouse border, spaced around 45cm (18 inches) apart, will let the roots spread around and down or you can plant into a 25cm (10 inch) pot or into growbags.

It is usually advised that you plant three tomatoes per growbag but this really does not provide enough compost. Take two 20cm (8 inch) or larger pots and cut the base off them. Fit into the growbag so the bag forms the base and then fill the pots with the contents of another growbag or just multi-purpose compost. Plant deeply into those pots and the roots will have more room to develop and the compost is less likely to dry out if you miss a watering.

With the growbag in position, pierce some holes about 3cm (just over an inch) above the floor level to drain excess water in case you over-water. Next, insert a small pot between the large pots which you can water into as well as into the large pots.

The final thing to do, however you plant, is to insert a bamboo cane by the stem. As the tomato grows, you will tie it to the cane to keep it supported.

It is critical to keep tomatoes watered regularly. In hot sunny weather they may well need double the amount of water to a cloudy day, so ensure that you have not just wet the surface of the compost. Irregular watering will cause the fruits to split and blossom end rot where the base of the fruit rots.

As the plant grows, tie in the main stem each 30–45cm (12–18 inches) up the stake and keep nipping out side shoots before they get above 3cm (just over an inch) long. These form at the joint between the stem and leaf. We are trying to get the plant to put its energy into fruit, not masses of foliage as it wants to do.

In dry weather, mist spraying will help the fruit to set. The only other thing you need do is feed the plant. Once the fruit begin to swell, use either a commercial tomato fertilizer as the instructions or liquid comfrey feed once a week. Do not over feed; it will not benefit you and can cause problems.

Once the plant reaches the top of the greenhouse or seven trusses of fruit have begun to form, pinch out the growing tip about two leaves above the last truss. Tomatoes grow from a special stalk called a truss. Don't confuse this with a growing side shoot when removing side shoots.

Stopping the plant at this stage will force the plant to put all its energy into the crop which will be ready before the season ends. The plant will react to this by trying to grow side shoots. Inspect the plant daily when watering and pinch out the side shoots.

Towards the end of the season, remove any leaves shading fruits to help ripen them.

Hygiene is important to avoid importing disease into the house, particularly potato blight. If you smoke, refrain from this in the greenhouse as tomatoes can catch a viral disease from tobacco.

For growing outdoors, choose the most sheltered and sunny spot you can. Start the seeds in the same way but in late March or early April, with a view to planting out in late May. If you can, pot on into 15cm (6 inch) pots and keep under glass a little longer. When planted out, keep under cloche for as long as possible.

With cordon varieties stop the plant after four or five trusses have formed. Bush varieties, due to the size of the plant, are usually best grown outdoors but because the fruit is often on the ground they are very vulnerable to slugs. Adding straw under the plant will help reduce this.

The chances are you will have some green tomatoes left on the plant at the end of the season. These can be ripened as described in October's guide, page 155.

Apart from pests and problems caused by irregular watering, tomatoes can suffer a magnesium deficiency due to the high feeding rate, locking out this micro-nutrient needed for utilization of nitrogen. The leaves will begin to yellow on the lower leaves and this moves up the plant. Treatment is really easy. Buy some Epsom salts from the chemist and mix 30g per litre of warm water. Allow to cool and spray the plants every couple of days, adding about 10g per plant into the water when watering.

The other major problem is potato blight which affects tomatoes as well. See page 117.

Sometimes you will find that the leaves have curled on the plants; this is actually nothing to worry about and tends to happen as the nights get cooler.

Tomatoes should not be grown in the same place year after year; there will be a build-up of pests and problems in the soil over a couple of years. If you're growing in the greenhouse border, change the soil, or at least the top 15cm (6 inches) each year. If you replace with good compost, the soil will be wonderful and the 'stale' soil will improve your plot elsewhere.

For outdoor growing, rotate the tomatoes. Strictly speaking, they are members of the potato family and should move as potatoes do but, in practice, they need the sunny spot so just avoid the same exact place two years running.

Turnips

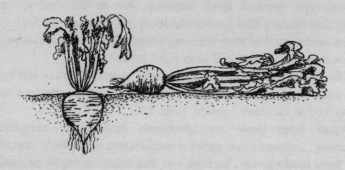

Fig. 74. Turnips.

The large woody turnips of old have mainly been replaced now with modern hybrid varieties that are delicious grated raw into a salad or as a welcome side dish, leaving the swedes to take over in the stew department.

They are a brassica so club-root is a consideration when deciding where to sow. They are a fast crop, being ready in just six to eight weeks from sowing to harvesting at the size of a golf ball or a little larger. As they grow on, they become less tender and flavoursome so successional sowing every two weeks will provide crops at their peak.

Sow thinly 1–2cm (¾ inch) deep and thin to around 10–12cm (4–5 inches) apart, either in rows spaced at 30cm (12 inches) or equidistant in raised beds.

Sowing can start as early as late February under cloche and run through to August. Maincrop varieties that are sown in July and August require a larger spacing (25cm/10 inches) to allow the larger root to develop for harvesting in November and December. Since the maincrop turnip is arguably less well flavoured and is inferior in minerals and vitamins to the swede, you may feel it only worthwhile to grow early turnips.

Apart from club-root, turnips are vulnerable to cabbage root fly so covering with fleece as a barrier may be necessary. Do ensure they are watered in dry weather or cracked roots and a woody texture will be the result.

GLOSSARY

Some of the more common gardening terms you might come across.

Allium   The Latin name of the onion family which includes onion, shallot, garlic, chives and leek.

Blanch   To deprive a plant of light to produce a tender growth as with chicory, celery and leeks.

Blight   A fungal disease, usually of potatoes and tomatoes.

Bolt   When a plant prematurely produces flowers or seeds at the expense of the edible crop. Most often affects onions and lettuce.

Bordeaux Mixture   A mixture of copper sulphate and slaked lime used to control blight in potatoes and tomatoes.

Brassica   General term for members of the cabbage family from the Latin *Brassicaceae*.

Chitting
(of potatoes)   Allowing the seed potatoes to form shoots prior to planting – see Potatoes, page 213.

Chitting
(of seeds)   Germinating seeds before sowing – see Sweetcorn, page 230. Also useful for establishing viability and germination rate of seeds.

Cloche   Any kind of (transparent) low-lying temporary shelter for use on open ground. See Cloches, page 45.

Club-root   Serious soil-borne fungal disease affecting all brassicas – see Club-root, page 113.

Coldframe   A low, glass-covered structure to provide sheltered growing conditions – see Cold-frames, page 47.

Compost   Term used for a growing medium produced by the decomposition of organic matter. Also commercial composts which include other materials such as peat or fibre, minerals and fertilizers, etc.

Crop
Rotation   Moving crops around to avoid the build-up of pests and disease and to best utilize available nutrients – see Crop Rotation, page 40.

Cucurbit   The plant family that includes cucumbers, marrows, squashes, pumpkins and courgettes.

Cultivar   A variety or type of plant; for example, Sungold and Gardener's Delight are cultivars of tomatoes.

Damping Down Raising the humidity in a greenhouse by watering the floors and/or staging. Tends to lower the temperature and reduce water loss from plants.

Damping Off Death of seedlings due to overly wet, crowded or poorly ventilated conditions.

Derris An insecticide of plant origin and so technically organic. It is non-poisonous to warm-blooded animals but deadly to virtually all fish and insects (including beneficial ones).

Double Digging A method of deeply digging over land, incorporating organic matter to increase the depth of topsoil, improve drainage and fertility – see Double Digging, page 30.

Earthing Up Process of drawing up loose earth around the stems or even over the foliage (especially potatoes) of plants to improve the crop and/or protect against frost.

Eelworm Tiny transparent worm which adversely affects yields and/or quality of several plant varieties, notably potato and onion.

Flea Beetle Insect pest that mainly damages radish, swedes, turnip and Chinese cabbage.

Fleece Horticultural fleece is a lightweight, translucent cloth that allows water to pass through and is used to provide shelter to plants and protection from pests.

Forcing   Process of making a plant grow in the dark to produce a tender leaf or fruit as with rhubarb.

Germinate   Not all seeds are viable, those that develop are said to germinate. Also the process of growing a seedling from a seed.

Germination   The number of viable seeds that develop
Rate   against the total number of seeds.

Gone Over   Term used when a crop has gone past its optimum harvest point.

Green   A crop grown to retain and provide nutrients
Manure   and organic matter in the soil to improve fertility – see Green Manures, page 73.

Hardy   A plant which is tolerant of frosts/winter conditions in the area in which it is being grown.

Haulm   The stems and foliage of a plant, usually used in regard to potatoes.

Heel In   Method of holding a plant in the soil for later use – see Leeks in December, page 163.

Heritage   Old variety of plant, usually harder to obtain
Variety   than modern varieties but often with fine flavour.

Legume   The bean family of plants noted for the ability to fix nitrogen from the air.

Module   Section or cell of an insert put into a seed tray to divide it up into separate pots – see Seed Trays and Modules, page 65.

Mulch   To place a layer of material on the surface of the soil. Usually to provide nutrients or prevent water loss or inhibit weed growth.

Offset   A short lateral shoot by which certain plants are propagated – see Globe Artichokes, page 197.

Pinch Out   The action of removing the growing tip of a shoot, to produce a more bushy plant, also known as **stopping**. Also the removal of small side shoots by using the end of the finger and thumb to pinch the stem until it is separated from the main stem.

Pot On,   The action of placing a seedling into a pot and
Pot Along   of moving a plant from one pot to a larger pot as it grows.

Riddle   Basically a coarse sieve made of plastic or metal to sift compost and soil.

Rust   Describes different fungal diseases by the appearance of orange patches that look like rust. Often affects alliums, especially leeks and comfrey.

Seed Potato   Small potato used to start the new crop – see Potatoes, page 212.

Set   Usually as in 'onion set', a small immature bulb which has been raised from seed before having development stopped by the grower. The resulting bulb is then *set* the following spring so as to complete its growth in one season.

Spacing
The distance required between plants to maximize the crop and efficiently use the space.

Station Sowing
Sowing of seeds in their final position. Usually two or more seeds are sown and then only the strongest seedling is allowed to grow on.

Stop or Stopping
See Pinch Out.

Successional Sowing
Method of sowing crops at intervals, usually every fortnight or three weeks, to provide crops ready to harvest over a period rather than in one go.

Tender
Describes a plant which is not tolerant of frosts or even cold weather in the area in which it is being grown. Typically requiring a greenhouse or coldframe.

Thinning, Thin Out
Removal of seedlings or small plants to permit others space to develop to their full potential. Because seeds may not all germinate, we sow more than required then thin out to the required spacing.

Transplant
To re-plant, usually, into final cropping position.

Truss
Used mostly with tomatoes to refer to the cluster of fruits on a stem. Vine tomatoes in a shop are more properly called a truss of tomatoes.

Tuber
The thickened portion of a root such as the actual potato in a potato plant.

Volunteer   A plant growing in the wrong place after self-seeding or re-growth of a missed tuber when lifting (main culprits are potatoes and Jerusalem artichokes).

White Rot   A serious disease of onion, shallot, leek, garlic and chives. It is soil-borne, very persistent, and can lie dormant for up to fifteen years.

Wireworm   Small worm pest mainly of potatoes, particularly troublesome when the ground is recently converted from grassland.

SOME USEFUL CONTACTS

My Website
All about growing vegetables and allotments with information, advice and chat forums.
www.allotment.org.uk

Organisations
Garden Organic
(formerly the Henry Doubleday Research Organisation)
Garden Organic Ryton
Coventry
Warwickshire
CV8 3LG
www.gardenorganic.org.uk

The National Vegetable Society
c/o National Secretary
Mr D S Thornton FNVS
36 The Ridings
Ockbrook
Derby
DE72 3SF
www.nvsuk.org.uk

The Royal Horticultural Society
80 Vincent Square
London
SW1P 2PE
www.rhs.org.uk

Mail Order Garden Equipment Suppliers
Two Wests & Elliott Ltd
Unit 4 Carrwood Road
Sheepbridge Industrial Estate
Chesterfield
Derbyshire S41 9RH
www.twowests.co.uk

Harrod Horticultural
Pinbush Road
Lowestoft
Suffolk NR33 7NL
www.harrodhorticultural.com

MANTIS UK Limited (For the Mantis Tillers)
Orchard House
Hempshaw Lane
Stockport
Cheshire
SK1 4LH
www.mantis-uk.co.uk

Wolf Garden Division
E P Barrus Limited
Launton Road
Bicester
Oxfordshire
OX26 4UR
www.wolf-garten.co.uk

Some UK Seed Suppliers
Thompson & Morgan
Poplar Lane
Ipswich
Suffolk
IP8 3BU
www.thompson-morgan.com

Suttons Seeds
Woodview Road
Paignton
Devon
TQ4 7NG
www.suttons.co.uk

Dobies Seeds
Long Road
Paignton
Devon
TQ4 7SX
www.dobies.co.uk

Specialist Vegetable Seed Suppliers
Medwyns of Anglesey
Llanor
Ffordd Hen Ysgol
Llanfairpwllgwyngyll
Anglesey
LL61 5RZ
www.medwynsofanglesey.co.uk

Select Seeds
58 Bentinck Road
Shuttlewood
Chesterfield
S44 6RQ
www.selectseeds.co.uk

INDEX

The main entry for each vegetable is in **bold**.